~~Bogo~~

Byro

Hope you

enjoy

Bob Barker

I'm In Cells

The captivating story of
Bob Barker
and the
Bob Barker Company

by Bob Barker

with Tony W. Cartledge

Bob Barker Company, Inc.
P.O. Box 429
Fuquay-Varina, N.C. 27526

ISBN-10: 0615643779
ISBN-13: 978-0-615-64377-9

Dedication

To my parents, Nally and Bell Barker, who raised me in a Christian home and taught me the values of hard work and passion for what's important in life. It was not until my adulthood that I realized how important parents can be in helping shape the values of their children as mine did for me.

Acknowledgements

Many people are responsible for encouraging me along life's highway and helping me to live this story. They are too numerous to call all by name, but I must list some who played an important role.

My wife Pat lived this story with me and made it a rich and a rewarding experience. We suffered through the hard times together, and she was always there for me whether days were good or bad. She always had faith in me and believed I could move mountains – and she laughed at my jokes. The good Lord put me at the right time and right place for her to become my soul mate. How lucky can a guy get?

My two children, Nancy and Robert, have been children that I have always been so proud to call my own. They have made my life complete by giving us four beautiful grandchildren. They are now taking Bob Barker Company to a higher level and following our lead in giving back more than you take.

To our dear friend and former pastor, Dr. Tony Cartledge, who played a pivotal role in helping us write this book, we are deeply indebted. When Pat and I were involved in starting Woodhaven Baptist Church, he came as our pastor and helped us build a thriving church with his caring ministry. He later went on to become editor of the *Biblical Recorder* (a North Carolina Baptist Newspaper). He is now a professor of Old Testament at Campbell University and the author of eight books and numerous other writings.

Our employees are our most important asset. Without them and their contributions, this story would not be possible. Many have been with us for years and are an integral part of the company. They have been the glue that sustained us through the hard times and encouraged us to keep on keeping on.

Nancy Mills was our Chief Operations Officer in the beginning. For years she brought great talent to the task and pulled us out of many situations that could have been devastating to the company.

H. T. Leary, my friend from Campbell University, led me into this business and I am grateful for that, and for his 26 years of service.

My brothers, Jack and Clarence, and sisters, Pauline and Shelby, brought a lot of joy to me with their interest and participation in the company.

Pam Williams has been my assistant for many years. She has played a crucial role in directing our community involvement while keeping me on schedule for hundreds of events and meetings.

Pam Whitmill brought great talent and enthusiasm, rising from an entry-level job through many levels of supervision to become Vice President of Business Development.

Ben Forbes, our Chief Financial Officer for more than twenty years, brought professionalism into our accounting system and convinced many bankers to lend us money. Ben passed away this past year and is sorely missed.

Stephanie Driscoll, who took Ben's place, has continued to raise our confidence in how we account for our business and in showing us how to give back.

Phyllis Wickham put our textile manufacturing on a professional level, and went on to help us in sourcing.

We have other long time employees who have been here more than twenty years, and they seem like family: David McKinnon, Sheila Staton, Melba Richardson, Robin Boraski, William Stewart, Debra Paddack, Melane Faucette, David Spivey, Neil McCraney, Shannon Pilkington, Maria Elena Gomez, and David Sears. There are so many more, and I wish I could say something about each one because they have all been a part of the success of Bob Barker Company.

Our outside board of directors, George Sneed, Dave Colburn, Gabe Cipau, and John Kasberger, with more than a hundred years of business experience amongst them, have helped put us right up there so that we've been able to compete with the best.

With the caliber of people we have been able to attract, how could we not be successful? I continue to learn from them every day and feel so appreciative of their deep love and devotion to Bob Barker Company.

I'm likewise grateful to all my friends at Campbell University, especially President Jerry Wallace and Vice President Jack Britt. They believed in me by placing me in so many important leadership roles, including Chairman of The Board of Trustees for three years, and honored me and Pat by conferring on us the honorary

Doctor of Humane Letters degree. Under their leadership, a small Baptist College, my alma mater, has been transformed into a great university, educating men and women in a Christian environment.

So much about my life has been providential: it amazes me to think back and see God's hand working in my life, placing me in the right setting, exposing me to the right things, and directing my path so that all these things came together. Some people would call it miraculous, but I see it as simple faith and trust in God.

Foreword

I am honored to write the foreword to the life story of my dear friend, Robert J. (Bob) Barker. Throughout my time as President of Campbell University, I have been blessed with the counsel, friendship, and brotherhood of Bob Barker. His steady and winsome leadership of the Board of Trustees has been the underpinning of one of the university's greatest eras.

Bob's biography, *I'm in Cells*, is a beautifully written and compelling story of how a child of the great depression, born to hard-working and godly parents, founded the largest detention supply company in the world. His early lessons as a child living on a Southern Cotton Mill Village, finding ways to make money for a soft drink or go to the movies, taught him if there is a "will" there is a "way."

Bob's "will" to find a "way" resulted in multiple vocational endeavors from selling Hope Chest China in Washington to designing, sewing, and manufacturing a comfortable and safe mattress for prisoners throughout the world. Although Bob's business interests quickly became national, he found time to serve his community and state with multiple terms as a mayor and as the first elected Republican state senator from Wake County since reconstruction. More recently, he has served his alma mater, Campbell University, as Chair of the Board of Trustees and campaign chair of the Convocation Center and Football Stadium Campaigns. His name is found on many places of the Campbell University campus, including the Bob Barker Residence Hall and the Barker-Lane Stadium. In recognition of Bob and Pat's love, support, and service to Campbell, the Board of Trustees awarded Bob and Pat the honorary Doctor of Humane Letters degree.

Bob and Pat's philanthropy has helped churches, towns, civic organizations, schools, prisons, prisoners, young people, and young professionals. As avid entrepreneurs, they embrace the necessity of hard work, a willingness to change, and informed risk taking to make new and renewed projects happen. When a new idea is shared with Bob, he smiles, and says "ALRIGHT!"

Anyone who knows Bob Barker soon discovers that his success is anchored by the spirit, counsel, encouragement, and side-by-side partnership of his wife, Pat Barker. Together, they have founded, nurtured, and grown the Bob Barker Company and had the trust and good sense to pass off its day-to-day operation to their children, Nancy and Robert. Bob and Pat continue to be close to Bob Barker Company and their valued employees and customers throughout the world.

Bob, I thank you for your smiles of friendship and your "ALRIGHTS!" They have made me glad!

Jerry Wallace, President
Campbell University

A Word from the Co-author

Assisting Bob Barker in the production of this volume has been a joyous experience. I've known Bob for more than 20 years and was privileged to serve as pastor to him and his family for 10 years. I thought I knew Bob well, but there was much I didn't know, especially about his early life, until we collaborated on this project.

The reader should know that Bob wrote much of this book himself, and in those parts my role was to tweak his stories for style and integrate them into the larger whole. Other sections of the narrative grew from interviews in which I would pose questions and then type furiously as Bob regaled me with stories of his childhood, college years, and early entrepreneurial adventures.

Box quotes scattered throughout the book derive from interviews I did with Bob's family and with long-term employees. Many of those quotations are highly complimentary to Bob, and he's a bit worried about coming across as blowing his own horn. Let it be said, then, that the employees freely praised Bob, without prompting. They clearly love and appreciate the man. Let me add that I chose the quotations to include in the book. While I understand Bob's concern about appearing prideful, I thought it was important for readers to catch a glimpse of how those who have worked with him the longest view the man who hired them.

I'm grateful to Bob and Pat for the opportunity to participate in this project, and I hope readers will find encouragement and inspiration for their own journeys as they read Bob's captivating story.

Tony W. Cartledge

Contents

CHAPTER 1

Clothing al-Qaeda

A rare snowstorm was just blowing into Fuquay-Varina on Jan. 2, 2002 when our sales office got a late phone call from Scott Air Force Base in Illinois. An Army contracting officer wanted 300 prison uniforms, and he wanted them pronto. U.S. military forces had gone into Afghanistan just two months before, trying to root out Osama Bin Laden and his al-Qaeda organization while also taking on their Taliban allies. They took so many prisoners, and so quickly, that they were having trouble managing them.

The base had ordered prison uniforms from us before, and they knew that if anyone could handle a rush order, we could – as the nation's leading detention supplier, we keep more uniforms in inventory than anyone else. We carried seven or eight colors, but bright orange was the most popular because it's so easily seen. So, when the officer asked what we would recommend, we suggested a basic two-piece orange uniform, a pullover top and pants with an elastic waistband, no pockets.

The trick is that he wanted the uniforms delivered to Fort Dix, in New Jersey, in time to be loaded onto a plane scheduled to leave at 2:00 a.m. on Jan. 4. That was nearly 500 miles away, and it was snowing to beat the band, but we took the order.

Nearly a foot of snow had piled up by the next morning, and it was still coming down. None of our freight carriers were making deliveries, and most of our employees couldn't get to work. My daughter Nancy, who had been promoted to president of the company just a few months before, put together a skeleton crew of three or four people. They boxed up the uniforms, along with knit caps, coats, socks, and step-in shoes. We got somebody to plow the parking lot and persuaded a trucking company to take on a special delivery. The army faxed security documents the driver would need to be admitted to the base. The order was on the truck by 1:00 p.m., and it rolled into Fort Dix twelve hours later, just in time for the 2:00 a.m. flight.

A few days later, I was watching a CNN report on prisoners in Afghanistan, and they were wearing our uniforms. I couldn't help but smile.

That first order was followed, in rapid succession, by several more. Within a week, we had sent 2,300 more outfits to Afghanistan in a routine sort of way, but there was another order that had everybody scratching their heads. A different army contractor had called Pam Whitmill (then Director of Sales, now Vice President for Business Development), and ordered large quantities of uniforms in various sizes – it ended up being 1,600 – also in orange.

The officer wanted caps and coats, underwear and socks, shoes and toiletries to go with the uniforms. These were not going to Afghanistan, but to a place called "Camp X-Ray," and we were given very specific instructions to put labels with "GITMO" in large letters on every box. None of us knew what "GITMO" stood for, but we followed the instructions. We didn't have to ship these: the Army sent a truck to pick them up and carry them to the Navy's port in Norfolk. Only later, as news reports filtered out, did we realize that they were bound for a new prison camp being opened at the U.S. naval base at Guantanamo Bay, Cuba. An MSNBC reporter who was covering the hurried preparation of Camp X-Ray displayed some of the orange uniforms that captured enemy combatants were expected to wear. Once again, we saw our merchandise on television.

It wasn't long before we got a second order for 400 more uniforms to be used at Guantanamo, but these were to be red, so camp personnel could use them to distinguish what they called the "really bad guys." Later, we got an order for 350 mattresses, which are engineered to be fire-resistant, mold-resistant, anti-microbial, and nearly impossible to rip open. That gave us an idea how many detainees they expected to house in what started out as open air cells with chain link walls.

As time went by, some of the detainees attempted suicide as a means of protest, and the army came to us again. We shipped them more than 800 "suicide blankets" and 200 "suicide smocks," both made of an extra strong, quilted material that can't be torn, tied, or twisted into a noose.

When I recall those days, though, what I remember most is that first hectic week when we shipped out 4,300 inmate uniforms and related supplies. Nobody else could have done that. We were not the only company in the country that sold prison supplies, but we were the one the Army knew could be trusted to fill the order, fill it right, and fill it quick. Bob Barker Company, then just 30 years old, had become the nation's leading detention supplier. How did we get to that place?

Well, it started with a bag of tools, and a boy barely big enough to carry them...

CHAPTER **2**

Cherryville

I got my first paying job when I was four or five years old. We lived in a small house in the mill village surrounding the Carlton Cotton Mill in Cherryville, an industrial town in the southwestern part of North Carolina. At one time, Cherryville was home to 13 textile mills, and some folks called it the textile capital of the world. Not a single one of those mills is still in business now, but there was a lot going on in the late 1930s.

A couple of our neighbors took an interest in me. A man I remember only as Mr. Wyatt was the night watchman, and part of his job was to go all over the mill at night and on the weekends. To prove that he had made regular rounds to check on things, he carried a clock with him. Different keys were placed at strategic places throughout the mill, and in each area he would use that key to wind the clock and show he'd been there. As we walked all over the plant, he would let me carry the clock and wind it at each station.

After I had been making the rounds with Mr. Wyatt for a good while, he began letting me make the rounds by myself. I was so proud for the chance to do something responsible that I didn't even think about the fact that I was doing his job for him, and I don't recall that he ever paid me anything. The mill would be dark except for a few lights scattered here and there, and it always seemed creepy to me. The wooden floors were always creaking and popping, so I carried a large flashlight and was constantly shining it in the direction of the noises, making sure that no one was sneaking up on me.

Hugh Sneed, our next-door neighbor, was head mechanic at the Carlton Mill, which was so close to our house that our address was 111 Carlton Street. Whether it was plumbing or machinery, if something broke it was his job to fix it, often at night or on the weekends when the mill was not running. Hugh had taken a liking to me, and called me "Lank," though I never knew why. I spent about as much time at his house as ours, and he would let me tag along with him as he repaired plumbing in mill village homes or machinery in the mill, whatever was broken. I helped to carry his tools, and he taught me what all of them were so I could hand up whatever he called for. And, if he was in the middle of something and needed a bigger Phillips head screwdriver, an odd-sized crescent wrench, or a new drill bit, he could send me back to the maintenance shop to find it and bring it to him.

He paid me just 25 cents per week, as I recall, but I learned a lot from watching him. I learned the difference between a card machine and a spinning frame, for example, and how each machine accomplished one step in the process of turning bales of cotton in to bobbins of thread. When making repairs, he would show me how cotter pins and other fasteners were used to hold things together. I'd watch him carefully take things apart and lay the parts down in order while he looked for what was broken or worn or clogged up. Then he would clean everything, replace or repair any broken parts and put it all back together with fresh lubrication.

I understood from watching him that most anything mechanical could be fixed if you paid close attention and had patience and were willing to put forth the effort. You had to be able to visualize how things fit and worked together, and I believed I could do it, too. Many years later, when I was buying broken slush machines so I could repair, refurbish, and resell them at a profit, I was using lessons I learned as a five-year-old barefoot boy dragging a bag of greasy tools.

Before my time...

My daddy was a talented worker and a respected supervisor at the Carlton Cotton Mill. He was over the card room, where machines stripped off slabs from the big bales of cotton, lined up the fibers, turned them into a loose rope called sliver, and coiled it into large cans. Daddy's name was William Rhyne Barker, but people called him W.R. He had left school after the third grade, but not because he lacked intelligence. He started working in the mills when he was 10 years old, and developed a real knack for understanding the workings of textile machinery. Daddy could listen to a machine when it was not running right and generally tell you what was wrong with it. He usually didn't even wait for a mechanic; he was more likely to jump right in with his own box of tools and fix the problem on the spot.

Skills like that don't go unnoticed, and Daddy caught the attention of the mill owners. He was made an overseer while still a young man, and he was able to pull it off because he was very good with people. He treated all of his coworkers as equals and they respected him for it. In this and other ways, he taught me to take responsibility for my actions, to treat all people with respect, and to give back to those less fortunate.

Daddy was so good with textile machinery that people who were starting up new mills or installing new equipment sought to hire him to get their mills up and running. For a short period of time, this led him to move the family (then consisting of Howard, Pauline, Clarence and my mother, known as Bell) from their home in Gastonia to the little town of Saxapahaw, on the Haw River between Chapel Hill and Burlington. B. Everett Jordan, who later served in the U.S. Senate for 25 years (1958-73), bought the old Dixie Yarns mill in 1927. He hired daddy to come and get it in good running order, at what seemed like the enormous salary of $45 per week. (Recently, Jordan's grandson oversaw a renovation of the old mill into upscale shops, restaurants, and apartments, but back then it was chockfull of factory workers).

Child labor laws weren't much of an issue in the 1920s, and my oldest brother Howard found some sort of job in the mill. Pauline remembers a day when Howard was paid a quarter. The family lived near a narrow plank bridge that crossed the river, and as he walked home from work, proudly admiring that shiny coin, he dropped it. The quarter bounced and rolled toward a crack between the boards. Before Howard could grab it, his hard-earned wage had splashed into the river. He sat down and started bawling, Pauline said, until a kind man came by and offered to give him a quarter to calm him down. Howard refused to take it, though. He said he wanted the quarter he had earned.

My mother worried constantly about her children crossing that rickety bridge, Pauline recalls, and always stood watch on the porch while they crossed it both on the way to school and when they returned.

Momma had much more reason to fear when my brother Clarence caught a serious case of pneumonia, which was often deadly in those days. She had lost her daughter, Helen at 18 months in Gastonia who died from pneumonia. One evening, I've been told, the local doctor came to check on Clarence, but had about given him up. As he packed up his black bag and prepared to leave, the doctor told Momma and Daddy there was nothing else he could do, but if Clarence lived through the night, he might make it. I've heard numerous stories about how all the neighbors rallied around and prayed for his recovery – and Mrs. Katherine Jordan, the mill owner's wife, was chief among them.

Clarence survived, but the family didn't stay long in Saxapahaw. My mother never liked it there, if the family lore is true, and maybe Clarence's near death had something to do with it, but she was instrumental in persuading my father to move back home to Gastonia. He didn't have any problem finding a job there, but his salary dropped from $45 to $17 per week.

My parents had met at the Arlington Mill in Gastonia, where my mother Bell worked with her sisters Cora and Josie. They had grown up around West Asheville, but the mills would send recruiting teams to the mountains, where they would entice young men and women to come work for them in the Piedmont. In my mother's case, nearly the whole family came. Her father had died but her mother, Martha Brooks, and her brother Romy also moved down and started working in the mills.

Daddy first started dating one of Mom's sisters, but the family thought he was too old (at 32) for her, so they pointed him toward Bell, who was about 22. He and Bell hit it off really well and he must have been struck hard, because it was not long before they were married. Momma's mother lived with my parents after they were married, and stayed with our family until she died at 86, when we were at the Dora Mill in Cherryville.

Life was hard in those days, and while they were in Gastonia the first time, both of my parents worked in the mill. They had two young children at the time, Howard and Pauline. The plan was for my daddy to work the day shift, usually 8:00 a.m. to 4:00 p.m., then Momma would work the second shift, from 4:00 p.m. to midnight. Daddy had better luck managing a whole factory floor of spinners and doffers than he did with Howard and Pauline, though. Pauline remembers that one night they gave him so much grief that he went down to the mill, brought my mother home, and would never let her work a public job again. He said they'd just have to find a way to live on one salary.

My brother Jack joined the family in 1928, while they were still in Saxapahaw.

The family moved from Gastonia to another mill in Lincolnton, where Bill was born in 1931. They had moved on to the Carlton Mill in Cherryville when I came along in 1934. Shelby Jean, the baby of the family, was born a couple of years later. My mother worked as hard in the home as my father did outside of it. She raised us to be thankful for all we had, and she did it with a wonderful sense of humor, even in tough times. She would often play jokes on us, and some of that positive and playful spirit rubbed off on me.

Village life

Mill owners typically built a small village of clapboard houses within an easy walk of the plant, renting them to employees at a reasonable price. It was good business, because it helped to attract and retain employees when few people owned cars. Since Daddy was a supervisor, our house was a little nicer than those built for the regular hands. Even so, our bathroom was on the enclosed back porch where there was a commode and a bathtub, but no hot water. We had to heat water on the stove when we wanted to take a bath, and there was no heat out there, so we didn't stay long in the wintertime.

When it got really cold, we would use a washtub inside the house, which was heated by a wood burning stove in the kitchen and a fireplace in the living room. We had to cut wood for both of them and it was quite a chore to keep an adequate supply to get us through the winter. I guess I may have learned something about planning ahead and managing inventory from that, and I'd always rather have too much than too little.

We kept all our perishable food in an icebox that was also on the back porch. Two or three times per week, an ice man would come by, and we'd signal him with a card on the front porch. Depending on which way it was turned, the card would indicate that we needed 25, 50, 75, or 100 pounds of ice. The ice man would chip off the right amount, carry it around back, and put it in the icebox.

My grandmother was still living with us during that time, and she raised chickens in the backyard. That allowed us to have eggs to eat, and usually a chicken for the table every Sunday. I didn't realize it at the time, but watching my grandmother decide how many eggs we could eat and how many should be allowed to hatch for meat and future laying hens showed me the importance of managing resources well.

We didn't have any sort of washing machine in those days. The mill had built a community wash house nearby. Local women would gather there and heat water in large iron tubs over a wood fire. They'd scrub their laundry against a washboard by hand, rinse it and wring it out, then hang it on a clothesline in the back yard. None of us worried about our underwear flying in the breeze, because everybody did it.

Daddy would use those same washtubs to heat the water we'd use to scald the hairs off of pigs he would kill in the wintertime. We'd cure a lot of the meat with salt and hang it in a building out back. We called it the smokehouse but I didn't understand why, since I never saw any smoke coming out of it.

The Carlton community was a great place to grow up because there were lots of kids around who were about my age, and there was a big open field nearby. If we weren't playing baseball on the field, we were likely to be out in the woods behind our house. There was a pasture between our house and the woods, and it was home to a notoriously mean bull. We would always check to make sure where that bull was before we took off running across the pasture, because he would chase us and scare the fool out of us.

We camped out in those woods almost every week during the summer. As kids, we thought of it as a big forest, but some years later I went back and noticed that the "forest" was a lot smaller than I remembered.

During World War II, a group from Charlotte came up and organized some people into a watch for identifying airplanes that flew over. I joined the group and got to where I could indentify almost any plane. I would take note of what kind it was, the number of engines, any identifying marks, and the direction it was traveling. Sometimes, we would camp out on the baseball field just so we could listen for planes, because we got to where we could identify them by the sound of their engines alone. We were supposed to call someone in Charlotte and report on what planes we saw, and I felt real big helping in the war effort.

I remember well the day the Japanese bombed Pearl Harbor. December 7, 1941 was a Sunday. Daddy and I were listening to the radio after church when the news first broke. We had no idea where Pearl Harbor was but knew it was our ships that were sunk and war was on the horizon. I was only seven years old, but I understood that my older brothers might have to go to war.

My brother Clarence did join up when he turned 18, and saw combat in the South Pacific. He didn't write home much, but my mother sent Pauline every day to the post office, about a mile away, to see if there was a letter from him.

I remember that when Clarence came home after the war, I jumped into his arms and was so proud that he was my brother. Like many veterans of World War II, he rarely talked about the war. The only anecdote I remember him telling is that once the bullets were buzzing so closely over their heads that he took everything out of his shirt pockets to get closer to the ground.

CHAPTER 2

War was not the only danger around, though. When I was about six years old, I remember wandering around some of the newer houses that were being built. A paint crew was coming through and painting all of them white. While walking through the house and talking to the painters, I saw a bottle of Dr. Caldwell's Syrup of Pepsin, which was marketed as a laxative. I didn't know that, of course. One of the painters dared me to pull the cork and drink the whole bottle, and I was always ready for a dare. I chugged it down, then spent all that night on the back porch toilet.

When it warmed up that year, my older brothers and some other boys decided to dam up a creek about three blocks from our house so they could make a swimming hole. They managed to construct a rather elaborate dam about 10 to 15 feet wide, and created a pool that was well over my head.

I had not learned to swim, and had been warned to stay away, but one day I was hanging out on the bank with my friend Galen Quinn. He pushed me into the water and I expect I would have drowned had it not been for a large root that extended from the bank to about halfway in the pool. I was lucky enough to catch hold of that root and pull myself out, but I never told my momma, for fear that I would have gotten a beating.

I later learned to swim quite well, and at a nicer place than a makeshift swimming hole. In the early 1940s Carl Rudisill, who owned the Carlton Mill, bought several hundred acres of land about three or four miles down the Lincolnton highway. He built a camp there for children in the mill village, and called it Camp Rudisill. It had nice cottages in the woods, each sleeping about a dozen kids. There was a large kitchen and dining hall where they served some great food – things I'd never had before. I'm pretty sure I ate my first cereal from a box there.

The camp had a large swimming pool. That's where I learned to swim, and I did so every day I could. I can't remember whether camp lasted for one week or two, but the first time I attended it seemed like an eternity, because I had never been away from home that long before. I can remember leading an expedition of other homesick boys who wanted to go home after several days, but nothing ever came of it. We all settled down and enjoyed camp life.

We exercised every morning, and I wasn't crazy about that because we did it without shoes, and the grass was always wet from the dew. Despite my love of swimming, I hated getting my feet wet. But we played lots of games that I enjoyed, and we'd sit around the campfire singing songs galore. I think that's when I started noticing girls.

Carl Rudisill was a generous man, and treated his employees very well. He later built a clubhouse and swimming pool for families living in the mill village. We would go there and take showers in the bathhouse every so often, since we didn't have a shower at home. I can remember that on the way in and out of the shower we'd have to step in an antimicrobial solution designed to prevent the spread of athlete's foot.

My feet encountered other problems, though. One day I was playing in the clubhouse, where a steam radiator used for heating the building stood by the wall. It wasn't connected to anything, and one day I started rocking it back and forth. I gave it one push too much, and it fell over on my foot, leaving me with several broken toes.

Our house was about a hundred yards from the mill's main office, and there was an open area shaded by large trees. Every July 4th, Mr. Rudisill would set up tables and haul in a truckload of watermelons and we would have a Watermelon Festival. In time, he expanded it to a celebration for the whole town on the school grounds. Later, he donated money to the school for a new auditorium and football stadium, both of which were named for him.

Self-reliance

Generosity went only so far when it came to salaries, however. Although my father was a skilled and valued employee in the mills, I doubt that he ever made more than $100 per week, and with seven kids to feed on that one income, there was precious little to go around. We learned early on that if we wanted anything more than the bare essentials, we would have to work for it and buy it ourselves – and we did. From the time we were eight or nine years old, if we wanted to wear anything other than worn out hand-me-downs, we bought our own clothes.

Scrambling for odd jobs did not cause us to feel put-upon or underprivileged or resentful: that's just the way it was. Work was a way of life back then. For me, it still is. I worry about children who have everything handed to them, and who grow up with no work ethic. When our kids came along, we didn't lack for enough money to provide for them, but we had them sweeping floors or emptying wastebaskets or doing other odd jobs at the business from the time they were in the first grade.

My older brothers got jobs in the cotton mill, making 35 to 40 cents an hour, and they taught me that I could work, too. When I was eight or nine years old, my brother Bill and I got jobs selling a weekly newspaper called the Cherryville *Eagle.* Being a paperboy was one of the best jobs I ever had.

The paper was a small operation that Howard Houser and his wife published every Thursday. The paper sold for five cents, and we got three cents for each one we sold. Bill and I were somehow able to claim the Carlton Mill area as our exclusive route and we would sell about a hundred newspapers every Thursday. That gave us a profit of about three dollars, which seemed like a massive sum in those days.

I learned the importance of knowing your customers. We became well acquainted with the people in our neighborhood, and we soon knew who had sufficient money and interest to purchase a paper. We would go house-to-house, knocking on doors. We never hawked the headlines as you see in the movies, with kids yelling "Extra, extra, read all about it!" We just asked, "Do you want to buy an *Eagle*?"

At the time, I had no inkling that I would own, edit, and publish a newspaper myself one day: *The Western Wake Herald*, in Apex, N.C. I did learn, however, that a paper could be written, laid out, and published by regular people. It wasn't rocket science.

Every Thursday afternoon we would go to the *Eagle* office in downtown Cherryville, next to the post office. We'd pick up however many papers we thought we could sell that day, then go out and start knocking on doors. The Housers were good, honest people. They trusted us to take what papers we wanted and to pay them after we finished our routes. We knew that meant we needed to be honest, too, and worthy of their trust, so we always kept an accurate count. I still believe business people should operate with the highest integrity.

Looking back, I realize that the state of the economy played a big role in our sales. The mill didn't always run five days a week, and if yarn or cotton was not selling and people could work only two or three days a week, then newspapers weren't selling either. There were times when people could not afford a nickel for a paper, and it hurt our sales.

Almost every Thursday, after turning in the extra papers and paying for the ones I'd sold, I would stop by the Dime store and buy something for my baby sister, Shelby Jean. It was a real joy to see her surprise at my gift, and it taught me something about the joy of generosity and the importance of giving back.

Selling newspapers also introduced me to the reality of competition, because occasionally another kid would intrude on our route and we'd have a turf war. I remember a boy named Harold Goldston who kept getting on our route and selling papers to our customers. Bill and I confronted him down at the general store one Thursday. We went after him, two-on-one, and told him to never come back to our route again. He didn't.

Outselling the competition as a multi-million dollar correctional supply company is not as simple as fighting out behind the store, but I learned early on that you have to take competition seriously. You have to work hard to find your place in the market, and just as hard to keep it, and even harder if you want to expand it.

My paper route was only on Thursday, so I looked for work on other days of the week, too. There was a general store not far from our house, and I hung out there a lot. I remember that they sold a lot of stuff, like soap powder, right out of the barrel. One day somebody (it might have been me) blew into the barrel and another kid got so much soap powder in his eyes that they had to take him to the doctor.

The store was owned by two brothers named Harrelson. They would give me odd jobs to do, and I took all they would give me. One of my main jobs was killing chickens on Saturdays. Meat was expensive, and most people couldn't afford to have it more than once a week, usually on Sunday. The cheapest meat available was chicken, so every Saturday morning the store owners would have someone deliver about a hundred live chickens, and we'd slaughter them for sale.

It was my job to wring the chickens' necks out in the tin shed behind the store. I learned how to grab the chickens by the neck, swing them around in a tight circle, then pull off their heads and throw them into the yard, where wandering dogs or cats would clean them up. It's not as hard or scary as it sounds: you just have to be confident and get a good grip. With a quick flip and a yank, the head comes right off. You didn't want to look the chicken in the eye or think about it too much, though, you just had to get on with it. It was a bloody, stinking job, but it felt good to be entrusted with such a responsible task.

The chickens would always flop around for a while, even without their heads. They scattered blood everywhere, but we just let them go while the blood drained. We kept a fire going under a big pot filled with hot water. When the chickens stopped flopping, we'd pick them up by their feet and dip them in scalding water to loosen their feathers. Then we'd pluck them clean, which was the hardest and smelliest part of the whole operation. With one quick cut, we could reach inside and pull out the entrails. We'd save the heart, liver and gizzard, and throw the rest out with the heads. Then we'd take the carcasses inside where the butcher would put them on crushed ice, and customers would buy fresh chicken for their Sunday lunch.

I also helped out with customer service inside the store, and delivered groceries, too. There were a few call-in orders, but most people walked to the store. They rarely shopped more than once per week, and they couldn't always carry the groceries back home, so we delivered. For small orders we used a bicycle with a big basket on the front, but some orders were too large for that. During the war, when the owners couldn't get gas or tires for the delivery truck, they bought a horse and built a stable behind the store. They cobbled together a small dray with two long poles and a two-wheeled cart using old bicycle tires. There was a single seat up front, and behind it was a bin about four feet long for the groceries.

After they taught me how to work the horse, I would dray groceries all over the place. When I stopped to make a delivery, I'd set a heavy weight on the ground and tie the horse to it so he wouldn't run off. Later, I would remove the harness and hang it up, give the horse a good currying, and feed him.

About that same time, Daddy got a deal somewhere and bought a cow. He was allowed to put it in the same stable behind the store, so I took care of it, too. That's where I learned to milk a cow, and it was a welcome addition to our diet, because I don't remember drinking much milk before that.

We were able to grow a lot of our own vegetables, because there was a big field near the store, and village residents were allowed to plant gardens there. We called them "Victory Gardens." Everybody respected each other's plot, and people often helped each other. We all tried to be as self-reliant as we could.

The general store also operated what we called a "dope wagon" in the mills, and my brother Jack and I worked those, too. Back then, everybody called soft drinks "dopes," because when Coca Cola was first marketed back in the 1880's, one of the ingredients was cocaine, which was legal at the time. In fact, Coca Cola was named for the coca leaves and cola nuts used in preparing it. Coca leaves, of course, are the source of raw cocaine. Coca Cola was invented by a pharmacist, and early on it was marketed as a patent medicine that would supposedly give users a lift and cure all sorts of afflictions. Southerners called it "dope," and they continued to use the term long after the company switched to using "spent" leaves that had the cocaine leached out of them.

All soft drinks were sold in glass bottles in those days, and there was a penny deposit on each bottle. One of my favorite things to do, even before I started working at the grocery store, was to comb the outdoor break areas where mill workers would go to smoke cigarettes and drink their dopes. It was easy pickings for me to collect the empty bottles they would leave and turn them in for the deposit.

Though everybody called it the dope wagon, the cart we rolled through the mill also carried snacks and lunch items. It was a sizable cart – about six feet long, two feet wide, and five feet high. The grocery store would pack cases of Cokes, Double Cola, Pepsi, RC Cola, and other soft drinks in ice down at the bottom of the cart. Double Cola was so named because you could get a 12-ounce bottle for the same nickel you had to pay for a six-ounce Coke: the same was true of Pepsi and RC Cola.

The upper part of the cart had racks filled with Moon Pies, candy bars, crackers, nuts, and sandwiches made at the store: mostly things like pimiento cheese, tomato, and bologna. Moon Pies and candy bars sold for a nickel, but we always had some penny candy, too. There were no regulations against smoking in the workplace or anywhere else, so we also carried cigarettes and plugs of Day's Work and Sparkplug chewing tobacco.

The store would fill the cart and load it onto the back of an old Model A truck. They'd back the truck up to the loading dock at the mill, and roll it onto the floor – assuming the truck got there. The guy who drove it claimed that one day, when he slowed to make a left turn into the mill, he looked to the right and saw his right rear wheel rolling by. But, they kept fixing the truck and making it work.

When I was barely big enough to handle it, I'd push one of those carts through the mill, making sales and giving change, learning who brought their lunch and who didn't, making sure I didn't overlook any good customers.

Through working at the grocery store, I learned a lot about the importance of giving good service and satisfying your customers. If you had about the same prices as another store but gave better service, customers would come back to you because they were treated better. I never forgot that lesson, and I'm convinced that customer service is a major part of what has made our business successful today.

Though I enjoyed the work, I knew that owning a grocery store was not on the list of things I wanted to do with my life. For a short period, though, my brother Jack and I did own a convenience store in Cary. If I had only known what all still lay in front of me...

CHAPTER 3

On the Dora

When I was 12 years old and in the sixth grade, the Dora Mill on the other side of town lured my father away from the Carlton Cotton Mill, so we moved across town to a neighborhood that everyone called "The Dora." They put Daddy in charge of the carding section, which was about half of the mill. Across the street was a loom room, where fabric was woven. It was the only mill in town that actually made cloth: most of the mills ran the cotton through a series of machines to open up the fibers and wind them into a loose rope that could be spun into thread.

One of the enticements leading to our move was the promise that the mill owners would build a new house for us to rent, and they did, at 103 Hicks Street. After a short time in an older house, we moved into the new place, and it seemed like a palace. That was the first time I lived in a house with an indoor bathroom, and it even had a central heating system. We thought it was all so great: there was a large yard where we planted a lawn with shrubbery and flowers, and an empty lot next to it where we put in a garden and raised chickens.

The house was about two blocks from the mill and company store, and about the same distance to our school, just on the opposite side of town. It seemed closer, though, since the area we walked through was more urban. Since I was three years older than my sister, Shelby, it became my duty to take her to school, even on the first day of classes. The only time I can remember my mother or daddy coming to the school was for my high school graduation.

We only lived in the new company house for about three years, though. My dad was nearing retirement as I entered high school, and we would not have been able to remain in the company house. Somehow he managed to scrape together enough money and material to build a house of his own while living on his meager retirement income. He did most of the construction himself, with help from friends and all of the boys who were old enough to help. We learned a lot about construction from that experience, and lived there during most of my high school years.

Fun without money

I remember playing a lot around the mill, especially on the weekends when it was closed. A warehouse where bales of cotton were stored made a great hideout for us kids. We liked to take the girls there and find ways to scare them.

We were also drawn to a drain tunnel that ran beneath one of the warehouses. It was about three feet wide, four feet tall, and about 100 feet long. It was dark, scary, and sometimes wet from the rain. It took a while, but we finally got brave enough to venture into it. We liked taking girls there, too, so we could show them how brave we were.

As the mill owners built new houses around the village we'd also watch the builders and explore the partially built houses after they went home. Once, as we played around in the loft of one being built near my house, I stepped through the sheetrock and created a big hole in the ceiling. Someone told the superintendent about it, and he told my daddy, who gave me a rather harsh whipping. It was the last whipping he ever gave me: he later told me he felt bad about it, but it was my fault and I still deserved it.

There was a patch of woods about as near to the house as when we lived by the Carlton, and it soon became one of our favorite places to play. We climbed trees and made hideouts in the dense undergrowth along a small branch that ran through the woods. Sometimes there was added excitement when a green snake would drop down our shirts as we crawled beneath the heavy vines. Sometimes the snakes had help.

I loved to hunt squirrels with my BB gun, and to check the boxes I built to catch rabbits. Killing a squirrel with BBs was generally a joint effort. We would climb a tree and throw firecrackers into any hole that looked like it might have a nest in it. The squirrels would run out, and then we'd shoot them. We usually had several boys with BB guns, and we'd have to shoot the squirrel numerous times because our guns were not very powerful. Today I'm sure people would consider such a thing to be awfully cruel, but we were looking for protein, and wild game was free. Whether squirrels or rabbits, we would take them home, skin and gut them, and have meat for dinner.

We didn't spend all our time in the woods, however. The Dora seemed sort of uptown to us, and as I entered my teens there were always reasons to go to town. As the new surroundings attracted me, I began to wander further from home.

Going to the movies, which we always called "the picture show," was often the thing to do. On many Saturdays, when we could cobble together fifteen cents for the price of admission, my brother Bill and I would hit the theater at one o'clock and sometimes we'd stay until five or six, seeing everything twice.

I remember one particular time that I wanted to see a show really bad, but I had no money. I was determined to see that show, though, and took off walking to town thinking that somehow I'd find a way. As I walked along with my head down, grieving the lack of fifteen cents, I had gone barely a block when I happened to see a dime and a nickel lying together so pretty, you would have thought they were planted there. I considered that to be divine providence, because I'd been praying up a storm.

Prayer proved less helpful when a boy named Galen Quinn – the same one who nearly drowned me at age six – and I decided we were going to build a motor-driven go-kart. I was 13 or 14 at the time, and we were convinced we could do it. We scrounged parts from machine shops around the mills, where it wasn't hard to find things like wheels, chains and steel rods. We found a gasoline engine, probably from an old lawn mower, to provide power, but we could never get the chain to engage correctly, so it wouldn't propel the kart. This did not stop us from pretending, however: we would push the contraption to a top of a hill with the engine running, then one of us would give it a good shove while the other one drove it down the hill. We would just wave at people like we had a real motorized go-kart. People thought we were so smart for building it, and we just loved it.

Bob of all trades

Life in the village always offered opportunities for some sort of recreation, but we knew there was more to life than play. Soon after we moved to the Dora, I was scrambling to create some income. We had an old push mower, and I'd go all over town cutting people's grass for whatever they'd pay me, usually fifty cents or a dollar, sometimes two if the yard was big enough.

In one of my first attempts at entrepreneurship, a friend and I worked at odd jobs and saved $10 to buy a pair of hamsters. Our plan was to breed them, raise more hamsters, and sell them. We had visions of getting rich off of our investment, and we were right in thinking that our stock would multiply quickly, but we had overestimated the number of people who want to buy a hamster. Three months later, we had so many hamsters that we couldn't give them away, much less sell them. My mother threatened to make me sleep on the back porch with the hamster cages if I didn't get rid of them.

I also got a job downtown, setting up pins in the bowling alley. They paid us five cents a game, and sometimes we could make as much as two dollars in a day, which was good money. We had some tough boys living on the Dora and I guess they wanted to test me. One in particular wanted to show me he was boss at the bowling alley, but I would have none of it. One day, it got so bad between us that the rest of the boys talked us into going outside to settle it once and for all.

I was one scared kid, but I was not going to back down because I knew if I did, he would try to dominate me like he did the other guys. When we got outside, though, I found out he was just as scared of me as I was of him. He backed down and said he didn't mean for it to come to blows.

One of the reasons I've been successful in business, I think, is that I'm in it to win, and I won't back down. The business world can sometimes be rough and tumble. You have to be tenacious, stand your ground, and defend your turf. You never know where friendships or positive partnerships may emerge, though. This same kid and I later became good friends, and he was my campaign manager when I ran successfully for president of the student body of Cherryville High School in the 12th grade.

Like many older children in Cherryville, I also picked cotton in the fall. One reason the town was full of textile mills is that so much cotton was grown in the area, and there were two gins in town to strip the seeds out of the cotton bolls. The fiber was baled and sent to the mills, while the seeds were saved for next year's crop. Cotton farming was such a big deal that they used to close the schools for about six weeks so children could help pick cotton.

We knew some people who raised cotton, and they would ask us to pick for them. That was some hard labor, and not my favorite job. We made only a penny or two per pound, and I don't think I ever picked even 100 pounds in a day. We had to wear a big cloth sack with a strap that went over the shoulder and the sack hung down, sometimes dragging the ground. It was rough on your back, bending over all the time and carrying that sack, and there wasn't much reward in it.

I still delivered *Eagles* on Thursday afternoons, and when I was about 14 years old, I added a daily paper route with the *Charlotte Observer*. With that job I had a list of regular subscribers, plus I could hustle and try to sell new subscriptions. Delivering a morning paper could be a rough job, especially in the winter when it was so cold and I had to get out on my bicycle, even when there was ice and snow on the ground.

To get my morning papers delivered, I'd set my old wind-up alarm clock for 5:00 a.m. and leave the house long before breakfast. I'd ride my bicycle down to the post office, where they dropped the papers off, and on cold days we'd sit inside the post office where it was warm while we rolled the papers and put a rubber band around each one. We'd pack the rolled papers in a bag, then put the bag in a basket on the front of the bicycle. Without slowing down much, I could pull out a paper and throw it onto each customer's porch. I took pride in being able to throw accurately and make the paper land just where I wanted it.

As part of my job, I had to collect subscription fees every week, but I couldn't always catch people at home. When people would put me off and I had to keep going back to collect, I'd really throw the paper hard so it would rattle up against the screen door and remind them that they owed me money, because I still had to pay for the papers, whether they paid me or not.

I don't know how I was able to keep up with what people owed me because I never wrote it down. Still, I could remember that Mrs. Jones owed me three weeks and Mrs. Smith owed me two. When I needed a little spending money, I would go knocking on the doors of my delinquent accounts.

The profit margin for the *Observer* wasn't as great as with the *Eagle*, but it was a daily route and the subscription price was higher, so I made more. Subscribers paid about 35 cents per week, and my cost was 20 cents. I had about 100 customers, so in an average week I would bring in about $35 total, and I'd make $15 or more profit when I could collect all of it. I had that route for a couple of years.

I took my job as a paperboy very seriously and made sure that all my customers got their paper every day. Even today, I occasionally dream about that paper route and wake up disturbed, worried that I missed someone.

There's one other part of that job that still haunts me, too. I bought a new Western Flyer bicycle with money I earned on the route. It was a beautiful, shiny green bike, and I think it cost nearly $100, which really was a lot of money in those days. I bought it on credit, and I don't believe I ever fully paid it off. I think I still owed the bike shop something like $20, which would be nearly $200 today. I hope they're not compounding interest on the debt...

I always looked for more full time work during the summer. I turned 16 and got my driver's license when I was in the 10th grade, and the next summer I drove a milk truck making deliveries in Falston, a small town near Shelby. Driving the truck, making sales, collecting money, customer service, and some heavy lifting were all part of the job. It required me to be really responsible.

I ventured further afield during the summer after 11th grade. Two of my friends, Wally Brooks and Bill Lackey, had graduated and gone to work with Winn Dixie Food

Stores in Charlotte. They let me come and live with them in a boarding house for the summer, and I got a job as a bellboy at the Hotel Charlotte. It was the leading hotel in downtown Charlotte at the time, with 500 rooms.

To work as a bell boy, the rule was that we had to pay the bell captain fifty cents a day. The hotel paid us a quarter an hour, but most of our income came from tips. Getting good tips was all about customer service, and I knew how to do that, so I made good money. My biggest tip came from a guy who was really drunk. He asked me to go and pick up his girlfriend from the bus station, so I met the bus and found his girl, then carried her luggage to his room. He gave me a hundred dollars. That kind of tip would be huge even today, but that was 1952, and I nearly flipped over it. I always wondered if he really intended to give me that much or if he was so drunk that he pulled out the wrong bill, but I didn't ask any questions.

I had started getting interested in politics about that time. I loved my civics class in high school, and enjoyed learning about government. That was probably the first year the Republican National Convention was televised, and I remember watching some of it on a TV in the lobby of the Hotel Charlotte. When I got back to school I ran for president of student body and won. I had no idea that one day I'd run for the North Carolina senate, and win again.

My senior year in high school was an interesting exercise in life with little sleep. I went to school, played baseball, boxed, and worked the night shift in the cotton mill. I would work from 10:00 p.m. until to 6:00 a.m., then come home for a short nap before going to school. I'd play baseball or box in the afternoon, go home for a quick supper, sleep until 9:30 p.m. or so, and then go back to work. I'm not sure when I did any homework.

Cherryville had just started a boxing team my senior year, and I just had to try it. I never was much of a street fighter, though I did once break my little finger when a boy in the bathroom called me an S.O.B. and I let him have it up 'side the head. I used a lot of bluff that tended to scare guys off or made them back off when they saw that I would not back down.

I remember several instances in high school when one particularly large bully who lived out in the country tried to start something with me. He probably outweighed me by 75 pounds and he was always pushing people around. We got into it one day on the way home from school, and I decided he was going to whip me or I was going to whip him. We fought out in front of the American Legion building. He would throw me down and I would get right back up and go for him again. Finally he got so exasperated that he held me on the ground and begged me to stop fighting. Not surprisingly, we went on to become good friends.

That was my secret. Even though that bully was bigger than me, I was in better shape and had more endurance. I think that had a lot to do with my success in the Golden Gloves. I wasn't a great boxer, but I had more energy or stamina than most of my opponents. I didn't smoke, drink sodas or eat junk food while I was training. I worked out a couple of hours and ran five miles down the railroad track every day.

I won most of my matches simply because I was in better shape than my opponents. We would box three rounds of three minutes each, but those minutes seemed like hours because the tension was so high in the ring and you had to be on your toes every second.

I remember one particular bout with a young man in Mount Holly. He had arms as big as my legs and he could hit as hard as a mule could kick. In the third round, he hit me so hard I was out of it, but managed to stay upright until the bell rung. When I got to the dressing room, I didn't even remember leaving the ring and had to ask someone who won. Needless to say, it wasn't me.

I actually had to fight under the name of Don Saine, a friend in my class, because I was just over the age limit of 17. Don was still 16, so I used his name, and the coach was just shady enough to let me get away with it. Once the *Charlotte Observer* printed a large picture of me boxing, with my back to the camera. The caption read "Don Saine lands a hard right to his opponent's head." I got a few victories in the Golden Gloves, but Don got most of the credit.

I might have won more matches if I could have concentrated on boxing, rather than working that full time night shift at the mill. My job was in the weave room, where thread from other parts of the plant was woven into cloth on large looms.

My job was to clean the looms between runs, and clean the creels when I wasn't working on a loom. Thread was fed into the looms from racks of wooden cylinders called bobbins, and they'd go through hundreds of them in a single shift. When the weavers changed out the bobbins, they always left a little bit of thread on each one. That had to be removed before the bobbins could go back to the spinning frames to be refilled, but it was too tedious to do by hand.

CHAPTER 3

Part of my job was to load the used bobbins into a bin and then pour them onto a ramp that fed into a machine that had a big spindle with four wooden paddles on it. As the bobbins rolled through, the paddles would catch the thread and strip it off so the bobbins could be refilled. Periodically I'd have to stop the machine and cut the waste thread off the paddles and put it in the trashcan, and if some of the bobbins were too tightly tangled for the machine to clean, I'd cut the thread off of those by hand.

When the weavers finished a run of cloth, I was responsible for cleaning the loom before they set it up for the next job. It was a terrible, nasty job, because they used a lot of heavy grease to lubricate the machines. The weave process produced a lot of lint, which would get embedded in the grease and become hard. I'd have to spray the whole loom down with a strong degreaser, blow it off with a high-pressure air hose, and then wipe everything down with a rag. The air hose was so strong that grease would fly all over me. I kept a pair of coveralls in the bathroom to wear when I was cleaning looms, and they would get so dirty and stiff with dried grease that they could stand up by themselves.

Working the third shift was really challenging. When I would stop to eat my "lunch" at about two o'clock in the morning, there were many nights when I'd almost fall asleep over my sandwich. It was often really tempting to close my eyes and just take a short nap, but I dared not because I was afraid I wouldn't wake up before break time ended.

I learned a lot from that job, including how to get fired – for the first and only time in my life. I knew it was completely my fault: one night I started horsing around with the air hose, pointing it at people or sticking it down their pants. The air was under such high pressure that it could have put someone's eye out. The supervisor said he couldn't put up with that, so he let me go. I said then I'd never be fired from another job, and I never was.

From all of these jobs, I learned important lessons about business, and how to make a profit. I learned that if I was willing to work, I could make money and not have to depend on someone else. With most of those boyhood jobs, I was pretty much on my own. When I was delivering papers, for example, I had to be self-motivated to get up so early on those frigid mornings. My parents didn't wake me up: I had to set an alarm clock. I got up before the sun, and usually didn't get anything to eat until after I'd finished my route. I learned that work is not always pleasant. It can be really hard, but also really rewarding. You have to do what you have to do, and give it your best, and find a way to enjoy it. If you have enough initiative and a willingness to work, you can make it.

CHAPTER 4

High Hopes and Hard Realities

From the time I knew what college was, I fully expected to go, even though none of my siblings had done so. In fact, I was the first in my family to even graduate from high school. I wish my brothers and sisters could have gotten more education, but all had their reasons, mainly a lack of funds. They had to work if they were to have anything.

I don't know how I figured that my parents could afford to send me to college. They helped me all they could, but by the time I finished high school in 1953, my dad was retired and only drawing Social Security. I think I got a $150 loan from the Cherryville National Bank to get me started, and I don't remember whether it was Daddy or I who paid it back.

Carolina days

I had my mind set on the University of North Carolina at Chapel Hill, which we all referred to simply as

"Carolina." Several of my classmates from Cherryville were heading there, including my friend Buddy George, who wanted to be a pharmacist. Buddy was always talking up Carolina, and he probably had more influence on my choice of schools than anyone else.

Buddy's aunt drove us to Chapel Hill that fall in her large and expensive Packard Motor Car. I remember that Buddy had almost filled the trunk with his stuff, while I may have had one box or suitcase. I didn't let that get me down, though. I was excited to be on my own as a college student.

When we arrived at Chapel Hill, I had not been given a room assignment, so the housing office put me in the basement hallway of one of their dorms. I slept there in a double bunk bed for a week or two, but finally was assigned to a room in Cobb Hall with a young man named Bobby Jennings, from Fairmont. We became good friends, though he transferred to East Carolina after that first year. Bobby was an education major, and he went on to become a teacher and later a principal in Fairmont.

Almost as soon as I got to Carolina, I went to the student aid office looking for work. Someone there lined me up with UNC Hospital, where I was assigned to the research labs of the Cancer Unit. My job was to clean the cages of guinea pigs used for experiments. It turned out to be one of the worst jobs I ever had. The animal cages were nasty, smelly, and confined in a stuffy space. But, I was paid 75 cents per hour for the work, and I could live on ten to fifteen dollars per week.

After learning the ropes around campus, I was able to leave the guinea pigs for a job at the snack bar near the Carolina Inn. The pay was the same, but the atmosphere was nicer and the work was a lot better than cleaning animal pens. The snack bar was a great place to meet and make friends with other students, who especially liked it when I gave them extra portions of ice cream.

Later on, I transferred to another snack bar on the east side of the campus. It was called the Circus Room because it was decorated with a large and impressive mahogany carving of circus animals in parade. The athletes usually ate in the Circus Room, where we made sandwiches and dipped ice cream for cones and milkshakes.

When spring came, we would get busloads of high school students visiting the campus, and it seemed as if every one of them wanted a milkshake. The ice cream was usually frozen solid, and I got a real workout on those days. Often I went back to my room holding my right arm because it was so sore from dipping ice cream.

I got to know a lot of interesting people there, including the first gay fellow that I remember meeting. He had been on campus for seven or eight years, taking graduate level courses every now and then. He was pretty smart, and occasionally helped me with some of my theme papers.

Bobby, my roommate at Cobb dorm, was a real sharp dresser who had some great looking sweaters and jackets. I remember a time when I met a real cute nursing student and got up the nerve to ask her out. When she agreed, I told Bobby about her and he said I needed to look sharp, so he loaned me one of his Cashmere sweaters. We were about the same size, and from then on, he would let me borrow clothes on special occasions.

Working at the hospital and snack bars helped me make it through the first year at Carolina, and I started thinking about a summer job. A fellow student tried to talk me into going to Wyoming with him to work on a ranch for the summer, the same ranch where the movie "Shane" was filmed. It sounded like a great adventure and I almost agreed to go, but my brother Jack offered me a job driving a Coble Dairy truck for him in Aiken, South Carolina, so I went south instead of west.

Jack had bought two trucks from Coble, and each truck came with rights to a sales route. We would buy milk and ice cream from Coble, load it into that cream and green refrigerated truck, and then resell it to stores, restaurants, or schools at a higher price. I worked a route in the Edgefield, S.C. area, and learned a lot about business that summer. I had to sell myself and sell my product, collect at every stop, and try to get new business.

I also got some of my first experience supervising an employee, an African- American man who rode with me and did most of the heavy lifting while I worked the sales end. It was still a very segregated world in 1954, especially in South Carolina, but we worked together, respected each other, and got along just fine.

I didn't drink or smoke while attending my first year in Chapel Hill, but while working in Aiken I picked up the smoking habit that I couldn't afford as a student. It took me 30 years to stop.

> Melane Faucette: *I started working for Bob on Dec. 1, 1989, on my birthday. I'll never forget walking into that smoke-filled room they were using for an office. The place reeked, and when I got home, I had to take a shower. One day Robin's trash can caught fire. For a long time, I was the only one up front who wasn't smoking, but when Pat quit, everybody*

> *else also had to quit, or go smoke outside. They started offering all sorts of smoking cessation programs to encourage employees to quit.*

I had a successful summer running the truck: instead of dipping ice cream, I was selling it wholesale. I was able to save some money before returning to school, and came back ready to go. My friend, however, didn't return from Wyoming until late the next fall, and he came back on crutches. He had contracted polio while working on the ranch, and he hardly favored the handsome, well-built young man I'd known before. I felt really sorry for him, but I also felt a lot of relief that I hadn't gone with him to that ranch, or I might have gotten sick, too.

My second year at Carolina seemed like even more of a financial struggle, maybe because I was also buying cigarettes. I got a job delivering papers through the dorms before daylight every morning, and continued to work at the Circus Room in the evenings.

I didn't work all the time, however. My friend Galen Quinn, a confederate in various adventures back in Cherryville, had come to Carolina as a freshman that year. He had an old Plymouth automobile, which we would drive up to UNC Greensboro. It was a women's college at the time, and my high school girlfriend had started her first year there. I didn't have enough money to visit her often, but she came over to Chapel Hill for a couple of football games and a dance during that first semester.

The academic side of my time at Carolina was challenging. I was not a stellar student, but I made decent grades. I learned early on how hard college could be when I tried to skip a course by challenging it. Carolina allowed entering students to bypass some introductory courses by taking a test to demonstrate that they'd already mastered the material. After arriving on campus, Buddy and I decided we would challenge college algebra. I had gotten pretty good math grades in high school, so I thought I had a good chance of skipping the course.

When Buddy and I walked in to take the exam, the test had been written out on three blackboards around the room. We took our seats and began reading the questions, looking for one we could answer. After straining our necks, trying in vain to find a single problem we could solve, we looked at each other and saw only despair. Both of us folded our papers and walked out the door telling each other that we'd soon be signing up for algebra.

I had taken French in high school, but the course was sort of a joke and I don't think anybody there ever learned any French. When I got to Carolina, we were told we had to have four semesters of a foreign language, and I immediately switched to Spanish because it seemed easier to learn. I remember sitting in Spanish labs for hours trying to get the pronunciation down pat, but to no avail. I finally got through three semesters, but I never took the fourth semester at any of the schools I attended. When I got to Campbell, Dean Burkot let me substitute Business Law for it.

I confess that I enjoyed sports more than academics while at Carolina. The tennis courts were right behind my dorm, and I took tennis as a Physical Education course one semester. I became pretty good at it, and later played a lot when I moved to Aiken, S.C., which was a big tennis town. Another semester I took golf in P.E., and that skill also came in handy when I was living in Aiken.

Every student at UNC had to pass a swimming test in order to graduate. I recall Buddy George having a tough time with it, and he may have had to take it several times. I was a pretty good swimmer, though, so I had no problems. There were other reasons to go to the pool, too. When we had a chance, we'd go watch the girls swim in the old wool bathing suits furnished by the school. The suits were extremely modest, but most of them were so worn that they had acquired holes in various places, which made for some very interesting viewing.

Though determined to finish college, I dropped out of Carolina after the first semester of my second year. The stress of working two jobs to support myself while also meeting the academic rigor required took a toll on me, and I decided to take a year off from school, thinking I could make and save enough money to go back and focus on my coursework. I had no idea that it would be six years before I got up the nerve or motivation to return.

An atomic interruption

I had a plan when I left UNC in the winter of 1955. My brothers Jack and Bill had been living and working in Aiken, S.C., and I'd spent the previous summer there, driving a dairy truck for my brother Jack. It just seemed natural to head back that way, because Jack had offered me a job and I knew I could stay with them until I got settled.

Aiken was a booming place at the time, because the federal government was nearing the end of a five-year construction project on the massive Savannah River Site, a nuclear facility built to produce the materials needed for atomic weapons, mainly tritium and plutonium-239. The Cold War was heating up at that time, and the escalating production of nuclear weapons required a lot of fissionable material. The plant eventually included five nuclear reactors and a number of support facilities.

Locals referred to the Savannah River Site as "the bomb plant," locally pronounced as "the bum plant." It was built on several thousand acres – 360 square miles in all – near the Savannah River, about 10 miles south of Aiken. Several towns and communities were taken over by eminent domain and the people were relocated to make room for the plant, so there was a lot of local resentment toward it – but there were also a lot of jobs.

The DuPont Company was running the plant under contract with the Atomic Energy Commission, and when I arrived in 1955, the facility was nearing completion. DuPont was hiring a lot of new workers and paying decent salaries, so instead of going back to the milk truck, I decided to look for a job there.

I applied for a position as a lab technician, even though my previous lab experience consisted mostly of cleaning up after experimental guinea pigs back at UNC Hospital. I was turned down at first, not because I lacked experience, but because a required physical examination turned up some sort of kidney infection. I went straight to a doctor, who gave me an antibiotic that cured it right up. I returned to the bomb plant a couple weeks later, passed my exam with flying colors, and got the job.

Since it was new and specialized work, we all had to be trained, so my lack of a college degree was not an impediment, at least for an entry-level job. The technicians overseeing the lab taught us how to analyze samples of uranium and plutonium, a task that had to be done day after day.

I enjoyed working in the lab. The company provided uniforms for us to wear, and everything was kept very clean. As an added benefit, quite a few people my age started work there at about the same time. We twenty-somethings all seemed to bond really well, and became fast friends both at work and after hours.

Analyzing mineral samples was challenging and interesting for a while, but it was the same thing every day, and before long I was getting bored. So, when I saw an opportunity to apply for a position in the Health Physics department, I applied for it and got the job.

Health Physics was responsible for measuring and trying to control radiation and contamination for all of the plant's employees. The field was still quite new, and we were responsible for figuring out how much radiation was allowable – then monitoring both employees and the environment to keep the levels in line.

The job provided me with a great learning experience, because I got to work all over the plant and the grounds. We were involved with every aspect of production and construction, research and laboratory work. This gave me a good understanding of how and why the company operated.

Even though I liked this job better than the lab, I still looked at it as just a job for the first couple of years. I was enjoying my life as a young single guy acting like a playboy, and my work was just a way to make money so I could afford to date, buy a car, and play golf.

My attitude toward the job changed, though, when I got a new boss. Lou Spano took a real interest in me and encouraged me to get more involved in my job instead of just seeing it as a routine exercise for eight hours every day. He gave my attitude a good course correction, and soon I became one of the hardest workers and most trustworthy employees that he had. I probably submitted as many safety suggestions as all the other seven or eight guys in the department put together.

With Lou's encouragement, I began looking for ways to make our work safer and more efficient. We worked in some dangerous situations, where radiation and contamination could easily overcome an individual, and I began to take it more seriously. He helped me realize that we were actually plowing new ground, still developing the technology and gaining the expertise needed to safely manage a workplace that was inherently radioactive.

Though the plant was built in order to make material for nuclear bombs, it also served an important research purpose, as the scientists and engineers there figured out how to harness nuclear energy to make electricity. In 1956, shortly after I started work there, two physicists at the site discovered the neutrino, which contributed to one of them winning the Nobel prize forty years later.

Overexposure is an intrinsic hazard when working with highly radioactive materials. As a protective measure, some areas of the plant had walls and floors that were three to four feet thick in order to keep radiation out – or in. All employees in the plant wore film badges, called dosimeters, that measured the amount and types of radiation to which they'd been exposed. In its most basic application, the film would turn dark in the presence of radiation: the darker the film, the higher the level. Part of our job was to closely monitor everyone's film badges, and to replace them when necessary.

We also measured radiation in other ways, often by doing what we called "smear tests." To check a surface for contamination, we would take a circle of filter paper and rub it against equipment, clothing, or even a person's skin. The paper would pick up tiny particles from the surface, which we could detect with a modified Geiger counter. We would routinely smear equipment and working areas for contamination, as well as areas outside the plant. With different equipment, we took countless air samples to determine levels of radioactivity in and around the plant.

The Savannah River Site was spread across an expansive wildlife area consisting of thousands of acres, with a tall fence around the perimeter. Security was tight, not only for vehicles and personnel, but even for animals: if a raccoon ate frogs from a contaminated pond, we didn't want it carrying that radioactivity into the community. Likewise, we checked the surfaces of cars and trucks coming and going. If they were contaminated, we'd have to put them through a decontamination process before they'd be allowed off the site.

It was also our responsibility to go into town and the surrounding area to take air samples and smears to check radioactivity levels. We never knew where the job would take us: once, when it was learned that a plant employee had been having an affair with his neighbor's wife, we even had to do a smear test on her to see if she'd been contaminated!

When decontaminating anything with a hard surface, we'd use the most absorbent thing we could find, which turned out to be women's sanitary napkins. Who would have thought that Kotex would play an important role in America's nuclear program? We bought them by the truckload, and could easily go through whole packs of six or twelve while scrubbing a floor or a piece of equipment.

When something became too radioactive to decontaminate, it was buried onsite in a special dump.

Decontaminating people held different challenges, because it wasn't enough to scrub skin that had been exposed to radiation: we also had to be concerned with radioactive particles getting lodged in a person's sinus cavities. If that happened, the affected employee would have to lean over a sink while a nurse sprayed saline solution into his or her nose and let it drain, repeating the process several times.

Some of the areas we tested were so highly radioactive that we used Geiger counters with sensors attached to booms that might be twelve or fourteen feet long. And, since our work took us into potentially hazardous situations, we had to take special precautions to protect ourselves from radiation. Though it seems primitive compared to modern protective suits, whenever we worked in locations thought to be "hot," we would wear assault masks or Scott air packs along with two sets of coveralls, shoe covers, a hood, and gloves. We'd wrap tape around our wrists and ankles, around the hood and the facemask, and at any other juncture where we thought air might seep in. I'm sure we looked like some sort of aliens or astronauts, though America's first space flight was still years away.

Wearing multiple layers of sealed clothing made the job even more difficult, because nuclear fission generates a lot of heat, and the temperature in much of the plant could reach more than 100 degrees Fahrenheit. Taped into our makeshift protective gear, we would soon be soaked in sweat and had to be careful not to stay too long, lest we become dehydrated.

This was one of the reasons I appreciated DuPont's shift system. We rotated three shifts, and they were arranged so that every few weeks we would be off for five days in a row. I had become friends with a pair of twin brothers who worked the same shift as me. When we had time off, we played a lot of golf, and it felt so good to be wearing shorts instead of that suffocating anti-radiation outfit.

Despite my young age and lack of a college education, my supervisors at DuPont entrusted me with a lot of responsibility. I had the authority to tell people how long they could work in a given setting. It was my job to identify hazardous and contaminated areas in the plant, and post warning signs or close them if necessary. I wrote reports and submitted them to a supervisor, but otherwise I worked independently except when we would have safety meetings and make our reports.

I learned a lot at DuPont. It was a very conservative company, and very interested in its employees. They paid us well, treated us well, and generally made us feel valued as a part of the company. I carried those lessons with me when I started my own business.

DuPont also gave its employees a lot of opportunity to do things on our own and make suggestions that would help improve or grow the business. I learned to adopt that as my own management style, giving employees a lot of freedom to think of ways to make the company more efficient or effective. Some of them have basically created new jobs for themselves by seeing a way to improve the business and then selling us on letting them do it.

> Phyllis Wickham: *There was a lot of opportunity, especially in the early years, because Bob would let you make your*

> *own job – you could pretty much create your own position and be as innovative as he was. It afforded you the opportunity to learn and to grow. You were allowed to make mistakes and allowed to grow. Once I screened 300 jump suits for Lexington County and made a mistake on them. I thought I'd be in big trouble, but H.T. sold them some kind of way, and saved me.*

I also saw DuPont as a company with integrity. They worked on a cost-plus contract with the federal government for a dollar a year, and they could have inflated numbers or run up really large costs, but they responsibly tried to make the work as inexpensive as possible for the government. I admired that. DuPont continued to run the plant until 1987, when Westinghouse took it over. A consortium of different companies runs it today.

While I was working for someone else's company those six years, I never entirely lost my entrepreneurial streak. During part of that time, my brother Jack and I decided to open a doughnut shop in a small shopping center, even though neither of us knew anything about making doughnuts.

I don't remember what we called the shop, but I do recall that Murray Wood, a friend I knew from First Baptist Church in Aiken, went out on a limb and signed a note for $3,500 so we could buy the equipment. He and his wife, Martha, became close friends when I lived across the street from them. When I got married several years later, Martha stood in as my mother, and Murray was a groomsman.

We opened the doughnut store having never made doughnuts before, but we found out where to buy the batter mix, read the instructions, and figured it out. We made a proofing box out of plywood and a light bulb, and once we got the fryer going we could turn out serious quantities of doughnuts.

Often I would go in at 4:00 a.m. and start making doughnuts before I went to my regular job at DuPont. Our brother Bill helped out, as did Jack's stepson, and we sometimes sold as many as 600 dozen doughnuts per day. On occasions, we'd make 500 dozen for the school to use as a fund-raiser. We tried to turn it into a Krispy Kreme, but were unable to get a franchise.

After a while, we decided to expand the store and add a bakery. I remember that we went to an equipment show in Columbia, S.C., and looked at a display of three-stack ovens. The dealer wanted $2,000 for them. We offered him $1,200, and after some dickering back-and-forth, he agreed to our offer. We went to rent a trailer so we could haul the ovens back to Aiken, but when we returned, the salesman who'd accepted our offer wasn't there. The man who had replaced him would not acknowledge the agreement and adamantly refused to let the ovens go for less than the original $2,000 price.

I've never been short on hutzpah, so I went straight to a telephone directory and called the first lawyer I saw in the Yellow Pages. I got him to call the company and tell them we were prepared to sue for breach of contract. The man didn't like it a little bit, but he finally let us buy the ovens for the agreed-upon $1,200.

We managed to install our new ovens, but neither of us knew anything about baking. We found a soldier from Fort Gordon who worked as a baker for the army, and hired him to come over and bake cakes, pies, and other things. The store never did make as much money as we'd hoped, so after about a year, we sold it to the soldier/baker on credit. He couldn't make a go of it either, so he later turned it back over to us. We eventually sold it to a woman who paid us enough so that we could pay off our original loan. Sometimes, I learned, you just have to recognize that something isn't working, let it go, and move on.

My life in Aiken was busy in other ways, too. I tried to go home to Cherryville to visit my parents every month or so. At one point, I persuaded them to come live in Aiken since three of their sons were there. I rented them a house and moved them down, but my mother never liked it or adjusted well. After about a year, I moved them back to Cherryville.

I rented a room from a lady named Mary Reager for most of the time I was in Aiken, though shortly before leaving I took over the payments on a house my brother had bought from the bank, and I lived in it for a while. While staying with Mrs. Reager, I became good friends with the Slayton family who lived across town. They had two daughters about my age, and I dated both of them. Mrs. Slayton became sort of a surrogate mother to me. I'd just show up for dinner two or three times per week, and they were always glad to have me.

Mrs. Slayton was really close to Jean Thurmond, whose husband was U.S. Senator Strom Thurmond. Sadly, Jean suffered from a brain tumor and died in 1960, and it had an impact on all of us. I've always been outgoing, and I got to know Sen. Thurmond quite well. He kept an office in Aiken, and he always had several pretty girls working for him there. I dated some of them, so I was around the office some. The girls would sometimes lodge with the Thurmonds in their home. One night Wally Brooks and I stopped by the house to pick up two of the girls, and Sen. Thurmond said "Ya'll don't keep those girls out late." I'll never forget that.

The Slaytons also had a good friend in New Smyrna Beach, Florida. When a buddy and I decided to drive to Florida once, Mrs. Slayton asked for a ride to New Smyrna Beach, and her friend insisted that we stay with them in their lovely home, right on the beach. They took us to a fancy party at a country club, where I met a wealthy couple, the Prices. The husband's name was Lee. I don't recall his wife's name, but I remember that she had some sort of crippling disease. Lee and I hit it off really well, and I went back several times, on those five-day shift changes, to visit with them. He learned of my interest in law school, and offered to pay my way if I would attend George Washington University.

It was almost time for the winter semester to start, and most students were already enrolled, but Lee, Mrs. Slayton, and I all flew to Washington, D.C. to see if I could be admitted on short notice. Senator Thurmond sent a car to the airport to pick us up and take us to the school, where I had an appointment with a friend of Mrs. Reager. He was working on a project to revise some textbooks that Mrs. Reager's late husband had written. It was late to be applying, but he helped me to get admitted.

I had not previously thought about moving north, but the offer of free tuition was too good to pass up, and with my growing political interests, life in the nation's capital seemed quite appealing. So, I started lining things up to leave my job at DuPont and move to Washington, D.C.

I didn't know it at the time, but my life was about to take on an even more amazing and wonderful turn, and it had nothing to do with making money or attending college. Shortly before leaving Aiken, my days as a playboy drew to an end when I met a beautiful young woman named Pat Mobley. Pat's home was just down the road in Augusta, Ga., and she was attending college in Columbia at the University of South Carolina. One summer she got a job working in the lab at DuPont. Ken, a good friend of mine, kept after me to meet this new girl. I put him off several times, but finally agreed to a blind date. He went with me to her house and introduced us, and I guess that was it. We liked each other immediately and started dating quite often.

Our courtship was encouraged by Martha and Murray Wood, good friends from First Baptist Church in Aiken. I had joined the church there, and had actually been elected as a junior deacon. Murray, the man who had taken a chance on me when he signed the note for our doughnut venture, took a special liking to Pat. He thought she would be good for me, and he was right.

Although our romance got off to a fine start, our time together was limited, because I was about to restart my college career – more than 500 miles away.

CHAPTER 5

If at First You Don't Succeed...

I had enjoyed the six years I spent in Aiken. I had a rewarding job, had begun to mature and settle down, and could have had a nice career with DuPont at the Savannah River Site. But, I'd never given up on the notion of finishing college. While still in high school and developing an interest in government, I had dreamed of going to law school one day. When offered a scholarship to attend George Washington University, I left my position at DuPont, put my furniture in storage, loaded my green Ford station wagon, and headed north to Washington, D.C. It was January of 1961.

College and the Capital

On the day I arrived in D.C., the city was pounded by the worst snowstorm in years. I parked on the street near the YMCA, where I was staying, and when the snowplows came by that night, they covered my car. I couldn't get it out for a week.

CHAPTER 5

I started out renting a room from a lady who lived near the campus. Her husband had been a professor at GWU before his death, but she stayed put and rented rooms to students like me. She was a real stickler for cleanliness: I remember that she changed the sheets on my bed every day. I later rented an apartment closer to downtown with a friend named Mike Monroe, who was an elevator operator at the capitol.

Mike's brother was a senior assistant working with Senator Henry "Scoop" Jackson, from the state of Washington. Jackson was known as an advocate for a strong defense. He was elected to the House in 1941, to the Senate in 1952, and served there until his death in 1983. Mike was a friendly sort, and with his brother's contacts and his own work running the elevator, he got to know just about everyone who worked in the capitol. He had become well acquainted with John F. Kennedy when he was still a senator, and liked him. By the time I arrived in Washington, he was President Kennedy, and Mike thought he could get us in to hear President Kennedy's State of the Union message in 1962.

Despite his many contacts and knowledge of the building, however, Mike was unable to get us in. We hung around outside the entrance until the whole thing was over, and finally gave up. As we reached the bottom of the long stairway leading from the capitol and turned toward the south end of the building, the president's limo emerged from an underground garage and drove slowly by, within 20 feet of us. As it did, President Kennedy looked over, rolled down his window, and said "Hello Mike!" We really felt like something special.

On another night that I won't forget, Mike took his girlfriend, along with Pat and me, to see parts of the capitol that most people never see. At one point he led us up a back stairway. We emerged onto the capitol roof, and walked all over it. With today's heightened security in Washington, visitors can no longer even get close to there.

As it turned out, my benefactor from Florida paid for only one semester at GWU and then left me to fend for myself, so I had to go back to work if I wanted to remain in school. I knew I was good at sales, so I found a job selling china and crystal for a company called Art Crafts. My primary prospects were young working women who were building up their hope chest. These days, it's customary for a woman to wait until she's engaged to be married before thinking about such things. She and her groom-to-be then choose what china, crystal, silver or other household goods they want, and list them on a registry. Friends and family members use the registry as a guide when buying gifts to be presented at bridal showers, and the couple can simply fill in what they don't receive.

Back then, however, such showers were less common, and it was customary for young women to prepare for marriage, whether they had prospects or not, by compiling a hope chest of things they would need whenever they set up housekeeping. China and crystal were always near the top of the list of desirable items.

Previously, I had sold things mainly on the force of my personality, doing what I could to convince people that they needed to buy the newspapers, milk, ice cream, or whatever else I was selling, and that they should buy it from me. Hank Gold, my sales manager in D.C., taught me to improve my sales by using a carefully thought out strategy designed to appeal to potential customers. We carried only four patterns of china and four patterns of crystal goblets, but Hank taught us how to sell effectively with only those four options.

The first step was to prospect during the day, finding potential customers and deciding which ones to call that evening, hoping they would let us come and show our merchandise. Our best sources of prospects were other girls, whom we referred to as "sponsors." When I would call a prospect, I'd mention the sponsor's name and say that her friend had asked me to call so I could show her our beautiful china and crystal. I would say that I was already planning to be in the neighborhood, and asked if I could stop by for a few minutes. Most of them would agree to see me.

At almost every appointment, the television or stereo would be blasting when I arrived, making it very difficult to concentrate on what I had to present. I don't know why people seemed to think the world would end if something wasn't blaring in the background. So, I would always ask if I could turn the TV or stereo down, and then I would just turn it off before sitting down to begin my presentation. I never had anyone to object.

Getting a girl to set her heart on one of my four patterns was an art, and Hank had taught me well. I carried samples of the patterns in a rather large case, with each pattern being encased in felt covers. I would start by building up my company and comparing it to others. I would explain that other companies and department stores would discontinue china patterns from time to time, and then emphasize that Art Crafts was always open stock, so she'd never have to worry about her pattern being discontinued. That meant she could buy as little as one plate, cup or saucer, and know that she could add to her set for as long as it took because the pattern would always be available.

I would then play up the idea that china and crystal was a good investment that would become more valuable as time went by. That wasn't necessarily true, but I believed it at the time. I never opened my case until I had made all these points and built up my prospect's anticipation to the point that she was really ready to see what I had. When I finally opened my case, I would expose only one pattern at a time. I'd let her handle a plate, looking closely, and getting the feel of it. Then I'd ask how she liked it.

After a while, I would set that plate aside and take out another pattern. I'd build it up, compare it to the first pattern, and ask which of the two she liked best. After getting her choice, I would put away the plate she liked the least, carefully wiping off the fingerprints and returning it to the felt case as if to emphasize its value. Pulling out the third plate, I would repeat the process, have her compare the two that were out, then put away the one she liked the least. I would do the same for the last pattern, so that she had chosen one of the four as her favorite. It didn't matter which pattern she chose, I would then really emphasize its fine points and congratulate her for having such good taste.

By this time, my prospective customer was usually sold on having china, and having that pattern, even though it might have been the last thing on her mind that morning. Before trying to make a sale, however, I would repeat the same process with the crystal, bringing out my four patterns of goblets one at the time, emphasizing their fine points, leading her to choose a favorite, and again complimenting her choices. Then I would try to close the sale.

I always got out a sales pad and put it on the table before I began my presentation. The idea was that she would get used to it being there, and not be as uncomfortable with it as she might if I had waited until the end. More often than not, I made a sale – and then asked if she had any friends who might also be interested in a call.

Selling china and crystal took me all over Washington, D.C., and there was no such thing as a GPS in those days, so I had to learn the street system really well. Before long, I became quite proficient in knowing how the city was laid out. I learned how to get from A to Z in minimum time, except that no one moved very quickly during the morning and afternoon rush hours, which went on for far more than an hour. Even in the early sixties, traffic was terrible at times, and tricky because some of the one-way streets would change directions during the day, with the traffic flow going into the city in the morning, then outward in the evening. I got caught several times going the wrong way, not realizing it was one of those alternating one-way streets.

Although I was pretty good at selling china and crystal, I could never get ahead. It took all the money I could make to pay tuition at GWU, buy gas, and cover my living expenses. I had stayed in touch with Pat that year, and was able to visit her a few times, but not enough to suit me. Pat had a friend across the hall who lived in D.C., and she invited both Pat and her roommate to spend the Christmas holidays in the city. Pat and I dated every night while she was there, and it was glorious.

Pat was finishing her senior year at the University of South Carolina, and as graduation approached, I had promised to attend. I really wanted to, but I just didn't have enough money to buy the gas. I waited until the last minute to tell her because I kept hoping I'd find the money somewhere, but it didn't happen.

Finally, I called to tell her that I just couldn't afford to make the trip, and I asked if she would consider coming to D.C. for the summer. She didn't have a job lined up yet, so she said that if I could get her a job, she would come up. That's where my acquaintance with Sen. Strom Thurmond paid off. I called his office to ask if he could help find a job for Pat, and by the next day there was a position waiting for her at the National Institute of Health.

The NIH had hired a bunch of college students to spend the summer coding questionnaires from a big medical study. Pat worked at an office in Silver Spring, Maryland, which is really a northern extension of D.C., just across the state line. She saw a notice there for a room to rent, and stayed nearby with a widow and her daughter.

Once Pat got to D.C., I wanted to spend every evening with her, but evenings were prime time for selling china and crystal to my target audience of young single women. So, I gave up that job, switched gears, and started selling door-to-door for the Fuller Brush Company. The primary customers for Fuller Brush products were married women, and at that time most of them were home during the day, leaving my evenings free for courting with Pat.

I was given a territory in Silver Spring, where Pat was living and working. I would drive into a neighborhood and park, then walk from house to house, knocking on doors. The main thing was to see how many calls you could make, how many people would allow you to come into the house and show your product.

People are a lot less likely to invite a door-to-door salesman to come in these days, but back then it was easy to get in the house by offering free samples, then go from there. If you were willing to do a lot of walking and knocking on doors, if you were good at talking your way in, you could do well.

I was determined to be an all-star Fuller Brush salesman. The guy who trained me said that I'd be a success if I could sell $100 worth of merchandise in a day, though it would probably take me a while to work up to that. I was determined to sell at least that much from the start, though.

The trainer said the average salesman could count on making a sale to one of every three customers he talked to. My first day on the job, I made 130 calls and sold $125 worth of merchandise, making a sale to one of every two people I talked to. Our cut was 50 percent of our total sales, and in 1962, that could make for a very profitable business.

We'd make sales calls on Monday through Thursday, then deliver the orders and collect payment on Friday. Silver Spring was a rather upscale area at the time, as most of the husbands worked in government. It sometimes took multiple calls to find people at home, but I didn't usually have any trouble collecting payment.

A Durham detour

Eighteen months in D.C. proved to be enough for me. During the summer that Pat spent there, we saw each other almost every night and I had fallen head over heels in love with her – but when her summer job ended, she was heading for Emory University in Atlanta, where she planned to work on a Masters degree in organic chemistry.

I wanted to be closer to Pat, and since my tuition sponsor had bailed, I had no real incentive to stay at GWU. So, late that summer I decided to move back south and start a business in Durham, N.C., while taking correspondence courses from the University of North Carolina. I had seen potential in the china and crystal business, so I worked out a deal with Hank Gold from Arlington, Va., my former sales manager with Art Crafts. Hank spun off his own business, buying Art Crafts products and reselling them to local franchisees under the name Quality Crafts. I obtained rights to the Durham area, which may have been Hank's first franchise. I started business as Quality Crafts of Durham.

I knew I wanted to be near Duke's East Campus, because it was a women's campus at the time. Most classes were held on the West Campus, but the girls' dormitories were on East Campus. A lot of young working women lived in the area, too, and I wanted to be close to my prime pool of potential customers. So, I rented a house on Lamond Avenue, just a few blocks away, and prepared to start making sales calls.

There was just one problem: I had no money, not even enough to pay for the merchandise I'd taken orders for. Hank would extend credit to franchisees for a short period, but it sometimes took our customers 12-24 months to make all their payments, creating a problem with cash flow. I started calling on banks, looking for one that would finance my sales contracts until I could save some working capital, but without any luck. After trying every bank in town, I turned to finance companies, and found one that would buy my contracts at 85 percent of the sale price and hold 15 percent in reserve until the customer had paid off the entire amount. Most sales were in the $250-300 range, usually for a four to eight place setting of china and crystal goblets.

To be truthful, Durham was not a very desirable place to live during the 1960s. Much of the city was run down, crime was rampant, and the city government was not doing much to make the city a friendlier place to live. Even though Duke University was a more upscale operation with about 5,000 students on the west side of town, students seemed to stay pretty close to the campus.

Durham is a long way from Atlanta, of course, so it was very difficult to see Pat, though we talked on the phone as often as I could afford it. I asked her to consider leaving Emory and transferring to Duke, and was overjoyed when she agreed. Pat moved to Durham in January 1963 and lived in a dorm that was just five or six blocks from the old house I was renting. We began seeing each other almost every day or night. My sales calls were mostly at night when prospective customers were home from work, but I always managed to get by her dorm and see her during the day.

Occasionally, when the weather was bad, Pat would ask me to drive her to class. At one point that winter we had a big snow, six inches or more, and she called me for a ride. It was treacherous driving, but she made it to her class. I don't remember now if I went back after her later or if she got back to the dorm another way.

I do remember, however, that we were deeply in love. I had proposed marriage right after she was accepted at

Duke, and she agreed. We had a rather short engagement and were married June 15, 1963 at St. John's United Methodist Church in her hometown of Augusta, Georgia. It was a rather large and really nice wedding, even though her parents were financially quite conservative.

Pat's grandparents on her father's side had been rather prosperous farmers, but lost most of their wealth in the 1920's when crop prices fell. So, even though her father worked in banking for most of his life, he wasn't keen on spending money. Pat overheard her mother telling her father that they should spend the money for a nice wedding, even if they had to borrow it, because she was their only daughter. Even so, both Pat and her brother Tom inherited their father's very cautious financial tendencies – and her conservative approach has probably saved us from going bankrupt several times.

After the wedding, we came back to Durham and moved into a brand new furnished apartment in Duke's married student housing. That was a great experience, and we were able to make some really good friends.

Our next-door neighbors were John and Marion Lock, from Canada. John was a divinity school student and a very interesting character. Pat was especially intrigued by his insistence that Marion arrange all of their canned food in alphabetical order, and by her willingness to go along with it. I was more interested in his approach to theology, which I thought was unique.

John argued that it was best to believe in God, even if God didn't exist, because the odds were better that way. I later learned that his philosophy was just a variation on Blaise Pascal's "wager" argument from the 17th century, an idea that John had probably read about in divinity school. In a book called *Pensées*, Pascal said that if you bet there's a God and you're right, everything's great. If you bet on God and it turns out you're wrong, you won't have lost anything. But, Pascal said, if you bet there is no God and you're wrong, you lose everything. It made for some interesting thinking.

Living with athletes all around us, we had little choice but to become Duke fans, even though my heart remained with the Tar Heels. For Duke, it was in the heyday of Coach Vic Bubas, who had some great basketball teams during his tenure with the Blue Devils. Pat was working as a lab instructor, and one of the basketball players was in her lab. She and I enjoyed watching them, though the Cameron Crazies weren't so crazy back then.

Being in the china business required me to be out calling on young single women most nights. That just didn't work out well for a married man, and the income didn't justify the disadvantages. So, I gave up the franchise and took a job as assistant manager of a department store in West Durham called Sawyer Moore. The store included a pharmacy, a photo-development section, and a broad line of goods common to department stores. In many ways, it was a forerunner of today's chain drugstores such as Walgreens and CVS.

Working at Sawyer Moore offered me some great retailing experience. I learned a lot about working with customers as well as how to promote and merchandise products. I also learned something about handling conflict and competition with fellow employees, for I was often at odds with another assistant manager who did not appreciate my creativity. I would build sales displays while on my shift, and he would come in and change them on his shifts. We were constantly in a running battle to outdo the other.

One might expect the store manager would have done some managing, but instead of helping us to channel our creative energy in a more positive direction, he just left us to compete. I learned from that, and I like to encourage healthy competition among our employees now, but it needs to be managed within a consistent strategy that maximizes profitability. The company's goals need to be more important than an individual employee's ambition, or opinions.

The other assistant manager and I rotated shifts, a week at the time, with one of us coming in early to open the store and get it running. I recall a wintry morning when the city had been hit with a big snow and ice storm on a day when I was scheduled to open. Travel by car was impossible, but I was determined to get there and do my job. I had to leave in the dark and trudge three miles through the frigid mess to do so, but I got the store open while most of the other employees stayed home, even though they lived closer than I did. Apparently, they had forgotten how to walk!

I remain a stickler about commitment to one's job, and have always expected our employees to show up for work whether it's snowing or not. We rely on catalog sales from 25,000 customers worldwide, and they don't care if the weather is bad in Fuquay-Varina, they just need our products, and we need their business.

> Phyllis Wickham – *Bob always gave us a long leash in figuring out how to do our jobs, but we were expected to come to work every day, even in snow and ice. He has a really strong work ethic, and expects employees to have it, too.*

Nancy Mills – *When Hurricane Fran came through in 1996, Bob was on the phone to me at 7:00 a.m. wanting me to get to work and get the phones up and running, but I lived a mile off the road and there were trees that had fallen across the driveway. There was no way I could get out, so I told him to get Dolan Johnson (a maintenance man who "came with the building" on E. Jones Street) to work on it. Everybody else in town was out of work for a week, but we were only down for one day.*

Melane Faucette – *When I was expecting my first child, we had some sort of special project coming up, and Bob wanted me to arrange to have the baby on a Friday so I could be back at work on Monday.*

One long year and two diplomas

Pat got a job with the Almay Corporation before she finished school at Duke, so we moved to Apex, where the company was located, in August of 1964. Her job focused on the chemistry side of developing cosmetics that were similar to other popular brands, but hypoallergenic. She continued her studies while working and completed her thesis in organic chemistry on something to do with N-amines, which I could not begin to understand. We had agreed that when Pat finished school and started work, I would go back to school and finish my undergraduate degree.

I needed 59 hours to graduate, and I had my heart set on starting law school in the fall of 1965, so I set about finding a way to cram two years' worth of course work into one. I re-applied to UNC and was accepted, but the school would not accept a number of the credits I had earned at other schools, and I had worked too hard for them not to count.

A friend told me about Campbell College. I had never heard of it, but I was a little leery when I learned it was in some place called Buies Creek. The school was only 30 miles away, but I had to look at three maps before locating it. Campbell had stepped up from junior college to senior college status in 1961. It's now a full-fledged university with several graduate schools and multiple campuses, but in 1964 it was a much smaller institution.

I came down and talked with the provost, Dr. A.R. Burkot, who was a legend on campus, serving on the faculty for 49 years before his death in 1984. Dr. Burkot was extremely helpful in patching together my previous credits. These included not only UNC and GWU, but also a few courses I had taken at the University of South Carolina-Aiken and at a University of Georgia extension site in Augusta. Dean Burkot also let me substitute some courses that didn't really fit (like Business Law in place of Spanish 4), and allowed me to take overloads that the average student would never tackle.

I took 18 hours both semesters, took a full load at both summer school sessions, and simultaneously enrolled in correspondence courses at the University of North Carolina. I would never have made it if Pat had not done the homework for the correspondence courses, though I still had to be familiar with the material and take the exams. As it was, I did not finish my last final until less than an hour before graduation was scheduled to begin that hot August day, but I made it. I'd been awake for three days, taking No-Doz and studying, so I was just about out of it when I graduated with a degree in history. We drove back home to Apex and had dinner before I had a chance to rest, and when someone passed me the mashed potatoes, I spooned them directly into my coffee! There's an ace student for you.

Since Pat had not put the finishing touches on her Master's thesis until that same year, we both earned diplomas in 1965.

I have always been grateful to Campbell for the way its staff helped me earn a degree during that crazy year. I've been happy that I could help Campbell in turn by serving on the Board of Trustees (including some time as chair), on a variety of important committees, and by contributing funds.

With a degree from Campbell in hand, I started law school at the University of North Carolina in the fall of 1965, and I thought my dreams had come true. We moved to Chapel Hill and lived in married student housing there for about six months, but before the year was up I realized that my dreams had been misplaced: practicing law wasn't really what I wanted to do. We soon moved back to Apex, and I was wide open for business... I just didn't know what that business would be.

CHAPTER 6

Papers and Politics

I've never been one to sit around when there are things to do and people to meet. During that hectic year when I completed my undergraduate degree at Campbell and the following year at the UNC Law School, I also managed to become quite involved with the Apex chapter of the Jaycees. The Jaycees are still around, though not as popular as in the 1960s and 70s, during their heyday. The name "Jaycee" is taken from the initials J.C., for "Junior Chamber." The national organization, the "United States Junior Chamber of Commerce," provides community service opportunities and leadership or management training for younger adults interested in business.

When I was involved, membership in the Jaycees was limited to young men from 18-35 years old (today the upper limit is 40), and there was an alternate program for women called the Jaycettes. We didn't think much about it at the time, but segregation by gender later became an issue when an increasing number of women wanted to join the businessmen in the Jaycees rather than being relegated to a supportive auxiliary club. Lawsuits against both the Jaycees and several other "men only" clubs led to a Supreme Court decision in 1984 that required the Jaycees to admit women, and the two organizations merged.

As community service, local Jaycee chapters would raise money for charities like the March of Dimes, or contribute to their communities by building playgrounds, parks, and the like. The Apex chapter sponsored the "Miss Apex" beauty pageant, and printed a program paid for by the sale of advertising. The pageant was designed to be a fund-raiser, but the chapter had never made much money because members typically sold only a few thousand dollars worth of ads, and spent most of that on the pageant.

When the other Jaycees learned that I had experience in sales from my years selling china, crystal, and Fuller Brush products, they asked me to head up the ad sales and put the program book together. I wanted to make a good impression on my new friends, so I took the job quite seriously. I called on every business in the area and solicited support from individuals, emphasizing the benefits of the pageant and the good causes it would support. As well as I remember, I sold somewhere around $15-20,000 of ads on my own. That was a significant amount of money for 1966, and five or six times more than the entire chapter had ever sold before.

I think I succeeded in making that good impression. I was named "Outstanding Young Man" for the Apex chapter in 1966, and the state Jaycees tapped me as one of three "Outstanding Young Men of America" from North Carolina for that year. Pat and I went to the national Jaycee convention in Detroit, thinking I would be in competition for a national award. When we got there, however,

I discovered that someone had dropped the ball and my name had not been entered. We still enjoyed the flash and dash of the convention, and filed away ideas that I'd later remember for trade shows.

Since Detroit is within driving distance of Toronto, Canada, we went to visit John and Marion Lock, good friends from our time in Duke's married housing apartments. Locating the Locks turned into quite an adventure, however. When we didn't find them at home, one of the neighbors said they had bought some land on a lake somewhere more than 100 miles from Toronto. On the strength of that information, and without the aid of an address, a cell phone, or a GPS, we found them. It took three days, some guesswork, and a lot of driving and asking around to do it, but we ultimately located them in a tent they'd pitched on an island in a large lake. I have always believed in perseverance.

In the news

Putting the Jaycee pageant book together had involved more than ad sales: I also had to design it, write much of the copy, lay it out, and follow it through the printing process. This was not an area where I had experience, and I got a lot of help from Cliff Blue, who owned the *Apex Herald*, a weekly newspaper serving the Apex community.

Newspapers rely heavily on ad sales if they're to make a profit, and Cliff was quite impressed with my sales ability. When I dropped out of law school at the end of the spring 1966 semester, he asked if I would consider becoming editor of the *Herald*. The current editor was leaving due to family concerns, and he needed someone right away.

CHAPTER 6

My previous experience in the newspaper or printing business was limited to selling papers as a boy and in putting the pageant program together. Although I read newspapers religiously and followed the news closely – especially with relation to politics – I had never given any thought to a career in journalism. I responded to his request with a whole list of reasons for not doing it.

Mr. Blue was a consummate politician, however. He had formerly served as Speaker of the House for the North Carolina legislature, and he knew how to strike a deal. He not only answered all of my objections, but offered me a half interest in the paper, knowing that this would fuel my desire to see it make a profit. This offer really piqued my interest and I could no longer turn it down: I had a chance to become the editor and publisher of a real live newspaper without a dime out of my pocket.

When I first took over the paper there were only two other full-time employees. A secretary/business assistant kept the books and looked after subscriptions, collections, advertising contracts, and other business matters. The other was a Brazilian lady, Jo Woodie, who wrote feature stories and some news stories. We had several correspondents who would send in newsy notes or announcements from their communities, though their only reward was seeing their name in the paper. I had to do just about everything else, including reporting on all the hard news.

My experience with the Jaycee pageant program had shown me that I could sell ads and do the layout, but I was hesitant about writing newspaper articles, even about happenings in the community. I had no experience in the area, so I began reading every newspaper I could get my hands on to figure out what made for good newspaper reporting. Before long I was reporting on everything from town board meetings to high school football games, and acting as the paper's primary photographer, too.

I took some of the photos with a 35 mm camera and built a darkroom where I learned to develop the film myself. The newspaper also had a Polaroid camera, and I relied mainly on it. I knew instinctively that people love to see their own picture or pictures of their kids in print, so I decided to use as many pictures as possible in the paper.

In another marketing move, I changed the name of the paper from the *Apex Herald* to the *Western Wake Herald*. The town of Cary was nearby, and had no local paper at the time, so I sought to broaden the market and increase our sales potential for both ads and subscriptions by aiming to cover all of western Wake County.

After a year, Mr. Blue gave me a chance to buy out the remaining half of the paper. I had to borrow $3,500 to make that happen, so I went to what was then Central Carolina Bank, which has gone through several ownership changes and is now part of SunTrust. The local bank officers were hesitant to take a chance on me, and took me to bank headquarters in Durham so I could make my case to the president of the bank. After our meeting, he agreed to the loan, and I became sole owner of the paper.

When I took over, the newspaper office was in a narrow but rather expensive building. I found cheaper rent in some rooms above the town drugstore and we moved there for several months, but when an old building on the grounds of a nearby car dealership became available at an even lower cost, I relocated the office again. Soon after, though, the car lot was sold and became Garringer

Chevrolet. The new management tore down all the old buildings, so we had to move again.

I found an aging but solid two-story storefront right in the middle of downtown, and paid $17,000 for the building, which was subdivided into 119, 121 (the upstairs), and 123 N. Salem Street. I couldn't borrow that much money from the bank, but the woman who owned it was willing to finance the sale. I agreed to pay her $1,000 down and finance the rest at six percent interest for 15 years. I still remember that the monthly payment was $126.53, because I wrote a check every month for all of those years.

When we bought it, one half of the building was home to the Apex Barber Shop. We put the *Western Wake Herald* office on the other side. The upstairs was divided into small apartments or rooms that people could rent.

The exterior of the building was brick, painted some very bland beige color, with a red, white, and blue barber pole attached to the wall beside the barbershop. At some point after we bought it, a truck coming into town lost control and ran into the front of the building, knocking out one of the main load-bearing columns supporting the upstairs. The upper level was sagging, so it had to be repaired, but I'd only purchased $15,000 worth of damage insurance. That wasn't enough to fix the structural damage and replace the brick, so we substituted wood siding and painted it a dusty Carolina blue.

The newspaper office was easy to move from place to place because we had very little equipment. We contracted our printing to a company in Aberdeen, about 50 miles to the south, so we didn't have to move a heavy printing press or stock big rolls of newsprint. This was well before computers became common, so our equipment consisted mainly of a few typewriters, an adding machine, a couple of desks and file cabinets, a typesetting machine and a layout table.

We would set the type and headlines with a machine that printed them in the appropriate column size, then use melted wax to stick each piece into place on a large sheet of paper lined off with a blue pencil. We'd patch in black spaces for the pictures, then take all the pages and photographs to Aberdeen. The printer would make negatives and drop in the pictures before making the plates that went on the printing press.

I'd usually take the paper down on Thursday morning and hang around while it was printed, pulling a paper every now and then to check for errors that could be corrected. Occasionally we'd have to stop the presses, make a change, and then start them back up. Once, I didn't realize until the entire paper was printed that the caption for a bridal picture had the wrong name. I knew I'd catch the devil for that, so I had them throw out the entire print run, fix it, and start over. That was my error so I bore the cost of it, of course – not a good way to increase profits.

When the printing was done, I would load the papers into my station wagon, bring them back to Apex, and personally put them in newsstands all over town. I'd take the papers to be mailed to the post office, which delivered them the next morning. The paper was coming out on Thursdays when I took over, but I later backed it up to Wednesday so weekend news and reports from Monday or Tuesday night town meetings would be a little fresher.

I published the paper for six years, even though it made very little money. If Pat hadn't had a steady paycheck, we certainly couldn't have lived off the profits.

That caused us serious pause when we talked about wanting to "start a family," as we say in the South – to have children. As one of eight siblings, I'd grown up in a large family and always liked the idea of having children. Before we married, Pat wasn't as sure about it, and then after we married, I worried about how we would support children if we had them. Though I was working hard, none of my business efforts were making much money, and we relied heavily on Pat's salary from Almay, where she had become one of their top cosmetic chemists.

We had bought an old house on South Hughes Street in 1967, and it seemed that every time we turned around, something needed fixing, and it was a constant drain on our finances. Still, a year or so later – after we'd been married for about five years – Pat brought up the subject of whether it was time to get into the baby business. I kept putting her off. I knew something about growing up as a child so poor that I had to find a job if I wanted to have new clothes. I couldn't envision how we could manage having children unless Pat quit her job, and I didn't think my income from the paper would be sufficient for us.

Finally, Pat explained that Almay would allow her to take maternity leave when the baby was born, and then go back to work. That assurance brought a new light to the subject, so I agreed that we should move ahead. Nancy was born in May of 1969, and Robert Jr. came along 20 months later, in January of 1971. They certainly brought a whole new dimension to our lives, and a very welcome one.

Pat took a three-month maternity leave after each birth before returning to work. We were fortunate to have a wonderful African-American lady agree to come to our home and care for Nancy, and later both children, when Pat went back to work. Mary Wilson had been helping Pat with the housework one day a week, so we knew her well and trusted her. She was wonderful with the children, and did much of the housework, too, though we couldn't afford to pay her very much. When she was offered a job at Cooper Tools in Apex, we couldn't compete with the salary, and didn't blame her when she left to take that job. Afterward, until the children started school, they stayed with another lady who kept a dozen or more children in her home and practically adopted them all.

Although we had worked out a way to have children and still survive financially, there was not much left over at the end of the month, and there was little prospect of the newspaper ever making us rich. One day in 1971, I was having coffee with the editor of the *Zebulon Record*, and the subject of buying and selling papers came up. He had bought a couple of other weekly newspapers, thinking he could combine some of the costs and make a consortium of small papers more profitable than any single one. I was surprised when he expressed an interest in purchasing the *Western Wake Herald*, because I hadn't thought about selling it. Not wanting to pass up a good opportunity, however, I pulled a figure from the air that I thought was way more than the paper was worth and put it on the table. He asked for some time to think about it, but soon called me back and agreed to the price.

The result was that I made more money from selling the paper than I ever did from owning it, but I was also out of work in two weeks, and with little cash to show for the transaction, because I had agreed to self-finance the paper's sale.

CHAPTER 6

Making news

While I was reporting on the news, I also started making news by running for public office. Writing objective stories about my own candidacy was a real challenge, but I always worked really hard to be fair in my reporting. When I had taken over the paper, I started attending all the town board meetings so I could report on town business, and I was a bit disillusioned by what I saw. I thought the town was lacking in good leadership, and I believed I could provide it. So, I ran for mayor in 1967 against an influential member of the town board. In a surprise to some, I won the two-year term in a close election. To the best of my recollection, it was by less than 20 votes.

The mayoral race was a non-partisan election, so party affiliation didn't come up. By the next election, however, it had become widely known that I was a Republican. As my contribution to the Republican cause, I had published some tabloid-sized promotional materials for various candidates. Since Apex was a Democratic stronghold, this did not go down well. One of the attorneys in town persuaded a Democrat to run against me in 1969 and made quite a campaign of it. I ended up losing that election by about the same narrow margin.

My father was one of the very few Republicans in Cherryville, so I had grown up as a Republican in a very Democrat-oriented town. Then I became one of few Republicans not only in Apex, but in all of Wake County. I helped to get the local Republicans organized, and our earliest Wake County Republican Party meetings were held in my newspaper office, with room to spare – we rarely had more than 10-12 people in attendance. The first Wake County Republican Convention was held in a lawyer's office in Raleigh.

The experience of operating the newspaper really whetted my appetite for politics. It gave me an opportunity to meet a lot of people in and around Wake County. And, it influenced me a great deal to run for the N.C. State Senate.

In 1971, the same year I sold the paper, I started thinking about running for state office, a dream I'd had since my interest in politics had blossomed in high school. I had been growing increasingly active in the Republican Party as well as in public service, so I felt prepared for the job. From 1970-71, I served as executive director of the Wake County Committee on Law and Justice, which was charged with getting federal funds to support law enforcement.

That committee had been formed shortly after the death of Martin Luther King, Jr. and the resulting riots that took place all over the country. About that time, the police chief in Apex died, his assistant spent time in the hospital, and several officers had left the force. We didn't want people to think there was no law enforcement in town, so a young radio dispatcher and I would ride around town in a police cruiser. If there had been a riot, though, we would probably have high-tailed it out of there.

While serving as executive director of the Committee on Law and Justice, I was able to get a number of grants from the Law Enforcement Assistance Administration (LEAA). With the help of a Duke law student intern, we wrote a grant that got us $1.5 million for a county-wide 911 emergency telephone system, making Wake County the second North Carolina county (after Mecklenburg) to have one. We brought in so much money for local law enforcement agencies that I actually had to beg sheriffs and police departments to take the money and use it to purchase supplies or new equipment.

While serving as mayor, I had been a delegate to the 1968 Republican National Convention in Miami, when Richard M. Nixon was elected as the nominee. Four years later, party leaders put me in charge of getting Republican candidates to run for N.C. Senate in the 1972 election. When I couldn't find anyone who would run, or who I thought could win, I decided to throw my own hat in the ring.

It was hard enough running as a Republican, but I had an additional obstacle in that one of my opponents was also named Bob Barker. To avoid confusion, I campaigned under my legal name, Robert J. Barker. One of my campaign slogans, plastered on signs around the area, was "When you vote for Bob Barker, make sure it's the right Bob Barker." Another was "Make your vote pay, vote Robert J."

I planned my campaign very carefully, setting out to contact as many potential voters as possible. I ran mainly on my experience as mayor of Apex, and that I had been chosen by the Jaycees as one of the outstanding young men in North Carolina. I knew how to get advertising and how to market myself, but I had to make a personal commitment, too. I worked twelve to eighteen hours a day for three months during the campaign. I had self-financed the sale of the newspaper with a personal note, so I went to the bank and borrowed against that note to pay the expenses of my campaign.

Over several months on the campaign trail, I developed strong confidence in myself and in my abilities. I learned that I could stand toe to toe with the best of my opponents by concentrating on my strengths and not my weaknesses, or even their weaknesses. I was determined to run a hard but clean campaign, and I did. On election night, before all the votes were counted, I went to bed confident that I would win. I first learned the results when my opponent woke me at 6:00 a.m. the next morning, calling to congratulate me on the victory.

The man I defeated was no slouch: he was chair of the Democratic Party of Wake County. With my victory, I became the first Wake County Republican elected to the Senate since Reconstruction: somewhere around 100 years. The district I represented included Wake, Harnett, and Lee Counties, so I had to cover a lot of ground to stay in touch with the people.

Serving in the Senate was not easy. The job offers part-time pay for what is often a full-time job. I was already working overtime with my brother Jack as we tried to get a fledgling business going. The children were young, and that compounded the need for a steady income. I became known as the senator with the youngest children and the oldest car.

So, I served the 1973-74 term and was grateful for the opportunity, but I didn't run for re-election. The country had fallen into a recession, and I couldn't afford to be a full-time politician. I had a business to attend to.

CHAPTER 7

In Search of Passion

After selling the newspaper, I pondered a number of possibilities for starting a business, knowing that I preferred to be my own boss than to work for someone else. I believed that I had the ability, the skill, and the work ethic to be successful. I had not yet discovered the business that would ignite my passion, but I was determined to find it.

My brother Jack and I talked several times about possible options. Jack, who was six years my senior, owned two grocery stores in the western part of the state, one in Dallas and the other in Lincolnton. Other people ran the stores for him, and he was always looking for some sort of sideline business.

Frozen ice drinks, sold under names like "Slushee" and "Slush Puppy," were becoming really popular about that time, and Jack thought there would be a big market for them in the Raleigh-Durham area. He suggested that we buy some of the slush machines and resell them to convenience stores and other businesses. It seemed like a good idea, so we decided to give it a try.

CHAPTER 7

Barker Brothers

Jack kept his home in Dallas, but would come to Apex during the week and stay in one of the upstairs rooms in the building I'd purchased, where the barbershop and newspaper were still located. We set up an office/workroom in a room behind the barbershop and started buying and selling the slush machines. We called our business "Barker Brothers," and used the trade name "Slushy" for the frozen drinks our machines produced. The year was 1972, and the first incarnation of the Bob Barker Company was open for business.

Working from the room behind the barbershop could be entertaining. There were two barbers. One of them, interestingly enough, was named Barker, and the other's name was Jack, so there were Barkers and Jacks working in both the front and back part of the building. Everybody knew that if you wanted to find out the latest news in town, you'd just go sit in the barbershop and listen to Jack talk while he cut hair.

Years ago, when most houses didn't have indoor plumbing, it was common for barbershops to have a couple of shower stalls in the back, and people would go into town on the weekends, pay a small fee, and take their weekly shower at the barbershop. The Apex Barber Shop had been around long enough to have that setup, and there were still a few people around who used the showers. It was an odd feeling to be back there doing deskwork or making repairs to a slush machine and look up to see a man walking by wrapped in a small towel.

We started out buying used slush machines, most of which were broken and had been relegated to a back room somewhere. I've always been good with mechanical things, and we knew that parts for the machines were available. So, by trial and error, we took machines apart and fiddled with them and learned how to repair or recondition them. If we couldn't get a missing part, we'd find a way to make it. By the time we replaced the plastic covers and spinning tops, the machines looked like new.

We could often buy used machines for as little as $100-200, and once we found someone who sold us a dozen old units for $1,000. After repairing and refurbishing, we could then sell them individually for as much as $1,250, which gave us more profit than the new machines, though we sold them, too.

With visions of becoming the Slushy king of the South, I flew to Keil, Wisconsin, hoping to talk my way into a franchise from the Stoelting Brothers to sell their machines in North Carolina. It quickly became obvious that I knew little about long distance travel by air. I left the Raleigh-Durham airport on a warm day in early spring, wearing a sport coat as I boarded the plane. When I arrived in Wisconsin, the temperature was well below zero, and I thought I would freeze.

The Stoelting Brothers operation was a family business that must have been unionized because they closed the whole plant for lunch. They didn't even answer the phone for an entire hour. The owners took me to a nearby bar where most of the management and employees went during the lunch hour. They'd sit there and have two or three drinks and then go back to work. I remember being amazed that a business could operate that way. I persuaded them to give the Barker Brothers the franchise for all of North Carolina, but since we were just getting started, they wouldn't extend a line of credit, so we had to pay cash for anything we ordered.

The problem was, we didn't have any cash to pay. So, I'd go to the bank and borrow $2,500, enough for two machines. The bill of lading for the machines would be sent to the bank, and the bank would pay the bill from the loan. Then we'd call the freight company and tell them where to deliver the machines.

Once the machines arrived, we'd load one of them into the back of my station wagon and go talk some convenience store owner into letting us set it up in his store on a trial basis. We'd stay with it a couple of days to make sure it was working correctly, and show the owner how much money he or she could make with it. Most of the time, we'd make the sale. We charged $2,195 for each machine, so by the time we sold the second one we could pay off the note and have something left over to pay expenses. Then we'd go back to the bank and start the process over again.

To maximize our profits, we also supplied the stores with flavored syrup and other things needed to use the machines. We had cups printed with the "Slushy" logo on them, and sold those, too. We'd supply the syrup and cups at no charge during the trial period, then sell them at a decent markup after stores bought the machine.

That led to one problem we didn't anticipate, one that illustrates the importance of doing sufficient research and knowing any regulations that apply to your business. North Carolina has a special tax on concentrated syrup used for carbonated fountain drinks or other similar purposes. Unfortunately, we didn't realize it applied to us until the tax people came knocking on our door one day. They wanted back taxes on all the syrup we'd sold, including the three to four gallons we provided to stores at no cost during the trial period.

My family of four brothers and two sisters. In this photo, I was about 15 years old.

Left to right, back row: Howard, Pauline, Clarence, Shelby, Bill, Bob, Jack

Left to right, front row: Bell Barker (Bob's mother), W.R. (Nally) Barker (Bob's father)

My graduation from Cherryville High School in 1953.

Here, I'm standing in front of the White House on Pennsylvania Avenue. This photo was taken in 1962 around the time of the Cuban Missile Crisis, and John F. Kennedy was the current president.

Our wedding party in Augusta, Georgia in 1963.
Left to right: Howard (brother), Carol Cassidy, Tom Mobley (Pat's brother), Mary Cochran, Jack (brother), High Mobley (Pat's father), Pat, Bob, Bob's dad, Arthur Wood, Ann Graham, Murray Wood, Linda Morgan Henderson

Our families at our wedding in St. John's Methodist Church in Augusta, Georgia in 1963.
Left to right: High and Flossie Mobley (Pat's father and mother), Pat, Bob, Martha Wood (Bob's stand-in mother), W.R. (Nally) Barker (Bob's father)

During the opening of the North Carolina State Senate, we were allowed to bring our kids on the floor for the first session. Here, I'm trying to keep Robert and Nancy, ages 3 and 5, entertained so they would not create a distraction. This photo was taken by the Associated Press and ran in almost every daily across North Carolina.

The remodeled front of our building on North Salem Street in Apex in 1984. The front of the building was all plate glass windows until a storm came through and blew them all out.

I am speaking to the members of the Fuquay-Varina Chamber of Commerce after receiving the "Outstanding Citizen of the Year" award in 1995.

Here, I am displaying my limited line of products in 1984 at the American Jail Association Conference.

Our son, Robert's graduation from the Wharton School of Business in Philadelphia in 1993.
Left to right: Shelby Barker Lowe (Bob's sister), Flossie Mobley (Pat's mother), Pauline Barker Levi (Bob's sister), High Mobley (Pat's father), Robert, Pat, Bob

Pat and I at Pat's graduation from Duke when she received her MBA in 1996.

Our daughter, Nancy at her graduation from Duke University when she received her Masters in Business in 1997.
Left to right: Dan Johns (Nancy's husband). Dot Jones (Dan's mother), Pat, Nancy, Bob, and High and Flossie Mobley (Pat's mother and father)

Cutting the ribbon to open our new corporate headquarters.
From left to right: Andrew Tate (Chamber of Commerce President), Robert, Pat, Bob, Nancy, Mayor John Byrne

Our Fuquay-Varina, N.C. Manufacturing and Distribution Center

Our Corporate headquarters on Main Street in Fuquay-Varina, N.C.

A trade mission to Dalian, China in 1999
Left to right: Wally Brooks (VP for International Trade), Elaine Marshall (NC Secretary of State), Bo Xilai (Mayor of Dalian), Pamala Davidson (Director of NC World Trade Center), Bob, Winnie Tan (Bob Barker Representative in China)

Part of our Ogden, Utah staff in 2012

BobBarker®

VISION

Transforming criminal justice while honoring God in all we do.

MISSION

By living our values and pursuing Bob's passion for customer service and innovation we are creating profitable growth and positively impacting lives.

VALUES

Integrity ❖ Service ❖ Excellence
Innovation ❖ Unity

Bob Barker Company Vision, Mission and Values

Bob Barker Hall is one of the most popular student residences at Campbell University.

Barker Lane Football Stadium at Campbell University

Our family at our retreat on the Cape Fear River in NC in 2012.
Left to right: Jenni Barker, Rob Barker III, Robert Barker Jr., Pat, Bob, Adelle Johns, Nancy Johns, Raymond Barker, Dan Johns, Rachel Johns
Photo by Chris Perez of Azul Photography

Pat and I being awarded the Honorary Doctorate of Humane Letters at Campbell University on May 12, 2012.
Pictured with Pat and Bob are Chairman of Campbell University Foundation Ed Gore (left) and Campbell President Jerry Wallace (right)
Photo by Bennett Scarborough of Scarborough Photography

Leadership Team of Bob Barker Company in 2012
Left to right, back row: Mike Reed, Jack Frankenfield, Stephanie Driscoll, Robert J. Barker Jr., David Sears, David Sheets, Jeff Fallanca
Left to right, front row: Nancy Johns, Kyle Martin, Pam Whitmill
(Dale Griffith: not pictured)

Bob Barker Company Team Members based in Fuquay-Varina in 2012

After adding interest and penalties, the tax bill they brought us was for thousands of dollars. I argued that we didn't know about the tax, so the penalties were unfair, and I refused to pay it. I fought that bill all the way to highest level of North Carolina's Department of Revenue, and they finally cut the amount to a few hundred dollars just to settle and be done with it.

The slush machine business started off really well, but when cold weather set in, it slowed down considerably, so we looked for other products to broaden our offerings. Kentucky Fried Chicken had become a hit with its pressure fryers, and some convenience stores had started including freshly cooked, hot food to their customers. We worked out a deal with a company that made pressure fryers and started selling them to convenience stores, too – along with cooking oil, marinade for the chicken, breading mix, plates or trays, and other supplies they needed to prepare and sell fried chicken and breaded potato wedges. As with the slush machines, we had to learn all we could about the products, demonstrate them, and then train employees in their use.

Seeing the potential profits offered by convenience stores, we also borrowed enough money to buy a little store of our own, on East Chatham Street in Cary. We wanted to call it "Happy Jack's" after my brother, but we couldn't use that because of trademark issues with Jack's cookies.

The store we bought was originally a wine store and was very run down, but we put a lot of work into it, converted it to a more traditional convenience store, and named it the "Happy Days Food Mart." We had visions of making substantial profits with that store, plowing them into others, and building a chain of stores that would make us rich.

During that time, I was also serving as a state senator and trying to faithfully represent my district. The senate required me to be present four days a week for about seven months of the year in 1973 and 1974. It was a hard row to hoe, but I learned early that if you want to be successful, you have to be willing to do what it takes and keep on keeping on. Often, I would spend the day at the legislature in Raleigh, then drive my clunker to Cary and work the night shift in the store. There were weeks when I hardly saw Pat and the kids at all.

Unfortunately, sometimes good ideas and hard work are not enough. Shortly after we got the store set up and going well, the town of Cary widened Chatham Street in a way that made access to our store very difficult. This cut our traffic flow so much that it was no longer practical to remain open for business. Without demonstrable success from that store, we couldn't get financing to expand, so our dream of owning a chain of convenience stores went down the drain. We closed the store and it sat empty for quite a while before we were able to sell it.

Jack and I had added a third partner when we started the store project. Richard Greer, who ran the store during the day, had been Jack's supervisor as sales manager some years before, when Jack had worked at a wholesale company that sold food and other products to grocery stores. As part of his job, Jack had started a private label (store brand) bread program to compete with the major bakeries, and it did really well. When he left to buy two stores of his own, Richard helped finance him.

Richard later left that company and moved to Raleigh, where he had hoped to start his own line of stores, beginning with our ill-fated effort. When that plan didn't work out, I had enough connections to help Richard get a job with the state, and he became the purchasing agent for youth services. By the time he retired from that position, we'd started supplying detention centers, and Richard came to work for us. Since he had ready-made contacts with all the juvenile agencies, he started out making sales calls to them. Later, he served briefly as sales manager for the whole company, but most of his work focused on juvenile agencies in Virginia, North Carolina, and South Carolina.

With the failure of the store, Jack decided to move back to Dallas full time. This was in 1974. Our business had little real value other than our inventory, much of which was bought on credit, so I assumed the debts and renamed it the "Bob Barker Equipment Company." Stage two of what would become the Bob Barker Company had ignited its engines.

Bob Barker Equipment Company

Our short-lived attempt to become convenience store barons had not been a success, but I'd learned a lot about the equipment and services needed to operate a store. As the convenience store industry continued to expand, I saw a ready market and began expanding our line of products to service not only the stores, but any other operation that included food services.

By 1975 I had hired someone to help with service calls, along with the first of several salesmen who traveled the eastern part of the state. Periodically, I would travel to Charlotte and buy a couple of retired fleet cars that Duke Power Company would sell at auction. That's what Pat and I drove, and I'd also provide one for the salesmen, plus gas money. We could buy the cars for a few hundred dollars, drive them several years, and usually resell them for close to what I'd paid for them. I couldn't pay the salesmen a salary, so they worked on commission, earning a percentage of all their sales.

We called on convenience stores, restaurants, correctional facilities, schools – any business or organization that used a commercial kitchen. My brother Clarence, who was nine years older than me, also moved down and started working with the business. I did all the paperwork and continued to make sales calls, but when a big sale came through, we all contributed to the hard labor of installing and servicing all the equipment. We added shelving, counters, stoves, and other equipment to our product line, and soon Bob Barker Equipment Company was set up as a full-service restaurant equipment company.

After the *Western Wake Herald* moved out of the building I owned on North Salem Street, we set up a showroom there, and eventually we tore down the dividing wall and expanded into the former barbershop, too.

About that time, we were also considering having Pat join me in the business. She had become somewhat dissatisfied with her job at Almay, where she had worked for 13 years. Pat was clearly the most capable chemist in her area, but she kept getting passed over for promotion to manager, with men always getting the position. She first raised the notion of coming to work with me, but I was very hesitant. For one thing, we relied on her paycheck to keep the business afloat: I would often go by Almay on payday to get her check so I could take it to the bank and pay some bills.

Giving up the security of Pat's steady salary was one thing, but I was also unsure what she would contribute to my equipment business. I wasn't convinced that she really wanted to do it, or that she could keep the business going if something happened to me. In fact, I was thinking that I needed a chemist like I needed a hole in the head. But Pat was much more than a chemist, and I soon learned that bringing her into the business was the best move I ever made. I've always been a big idea man, a dreamer, but not as good with organization and planning. It turned out that Pat had all of that covered.

I have never been afraid of taking a risk, so we agreed to a plan in which Pat quit her job and came to work in the business in September 1977. It soon became apparent that when we combined Pat's left-brain analytical skills and conservative sensibility with the fertile chaos of my right-brain creativity and my drive to succeed, we really had something. When I saw the stability and order she brought to the company, I wished I had asked her to work with me sooner. As the years went by and our business expanded, Pat was able to keep a tight rein on some of my more impulsive notions, and probably kept us from going bankrupt more than once.

> Pat Barker – *I had a hard time giving up the security of a paycheck, but I decided the worst that could happen was that we could go bankrupt, and I could live with that. Fortunately, we never did. Our team members have often noted how well matched Bob and I are in that he's always dreaming about new products or business schemes, while I'm attend-*

ing to the bottom line. It took me forever to learn, though, that when Bob really wants to do something, no amount of facts and figures will convince him otherwise.

Debbie Paddack – *I've always looked at Bob like a helium-filled balloon on a long string bouncing around the air, with Pat always pulling on the string and trying to rein him in.*

Pam Whitmill – *Bob grew the company, and Pat kept it profitable.*

Whenever I get a chance to talk to students or young entrepreneurs, I always emphasize the importance of your spouse being supportive of your career, someone who shares your goals. Even before she came to work with me, Pat encouraged me in whatever I was doing, and didn't complain when I'd use part of her paycheck to pay a bill that my business owed. Not every couple has the complementary business skills or personalities that would enable them to work together as Pat and I have. Still, whether you both work in the business or not, any businessperson who is married will have a better chance of success if his or her partner supports the business.

By the time we had the showroom set up, Nancy and Robert were in school at A. V. Baucom Elementary School, about a mile away. Every afternoon they would join a group of other children who walked home from school, except they walked to our showroom. We gave them odd jobs around the store and paid them a little bit.

That practice served a number of purposes: the children learned responsibility, they earned a little money, we got to spend time together as a family, and we didn't have to pay anyone for childcare!

> Robert Barker, Jr. – *We'd work in the showroom every day after school. I remember emptying the ashtrays, which was a real job because just about everybody smoked. I carried out the trash, dusted all the equipment that was on display, filed catalogs from suppliers on the shelves, things like that. I'd occasionally tag along with Dad or a service man when they were repairing an ice machine, carrying the tools and fetching things for them.*
>
> *I remember spending a lot of my money at the arcade up the street, or buying Orange-Ade and ham & cheese sandwiches from the drugstore, which had a lunch counter. But, I also made regular deposits at Raleigh Federal Savings & Loan, just a couple of doors down from the showroom.*
>
> Nancy Barker – *We were paid $10 per week, which really wasn't bad back then. I loved shopping and spent most of my money, but Robert saved most of his. We cleaned and did odd jobs around the showroom, but my favorite thing was*

> *that sometimes, especially on Saturdays, they would set up one of the Slushy machines on the sidewalk and let us run it like an upscale lemonade stand. My friends would come and help and we'd drink so many Slushies that we probably didn't make any profits, but we had a lot of fun.*

To grow the business, we had to compete with established firms in Raleigh like Montgomery Green (no longer in business) and United Restaurant Equipment Company. Some popular manufacturers, like Hobart, wouldn't sell to us, but others would. We sold a lot of equipment to restaurants, did bid work for schools, and did our best to capitalize on all the building going on at Research Triangle Park, which was really on the upswing about that time.

One of our more memorable jobs was for IBM, which was expanding its facilities in RTP in a major way. They contracted with us to build a fancy serving line for a posh dining room in one of their buildings. The thing was, they wanted us to encase the serving bar with a particular type of oak paneling that was very expensive, maybe $80 per sheet. I didn't really want to do it because we didn't normally do carpentry and cabinet work, and I would have to subcontract that part of the job. So, I threw out a really high price that I thought they'd surely turn down. To my surprise, they didn't blink, but told us to go ahead and do it.

I was able to find a cabinet-maker in Apex who did a nice job of building the case for us and installing it in IBM's dining room. We had overestimated the amount of oak paneling needed, though. There were probably 25-30 sheets left over, so I stored it in the warehouse and some years later, when we'd bought a newer house on the outskirts of Apex, I paneled the entire basement with some really expensive oak.

As the business continued to grow, we kept adding products, including kitchen utensils, pots and pans, silverware, plates, tables and tablecloths – if you could use it in a restaurant, we sold it. The building at 123 N. Salem Street began to grow cramped, and we looked around for a larger and more attractive space. A furniture store down the street at 225 N. Salem St. became available, so in 1978 we rented it and were able to set up a more professional looking showroom area.

The business grew slowly but steadily for the next couple of years, as we competed for and began to win contracts with the government, schools, correctional institutions, hospitals, and private restaurants. We added more salesmen to comb the highways and back roads of eastern North Carolina in search of more opportunities including jails and local government facilities, and in 1979 we added someone to help us in the office.

We got a big boost when we got an exclusive franchise from Ross-Temp, a leading manufacturer of icemakers, for about half the state. About the same time we won a contract from North Carolina to supply certain sizes of icemakers for the entire state. As a result, we were ordering icemakers by the truckload and delivering them on a regular basis. We needed more space to store them, so we continued to expand our footprint in downtown Apex. In 1981 we purchased the old Garringer Chevrolet dealership two doors over, obtaining an even nicer showroom with large plate glass windows, plus lots of warehouse space in the former garage and a hefty elevator to access an upstairs area. In time we took over the space formerly occupied by a hardware store on one side of us and a fertilizer warehouse on the other, giving us a total of about 40,000 square feet of commercial space.

Although our main business was supplying restaurant equipment to anyone who had a commercial kitchen, our experience with stand-alone restaurants was mixed. Occasionally we would have a well-financed customer who would have us set up the entire kitchen, but more often our restaurant customers bought stoves, coolers, dishwashers and the like one piece at a time. Sometimes they got financing from the bank, and sometimes we held the paper.

This often became a problem because with few exceptions, profit margins in the restaurant business are slim, and many people who love the idea of running a restaurant don't have the business savvy or the financial discipline to operate them profitably. When they go belly up, especially if they file for bankruptcy, their creditors lose out. Once, before we understood the bankruptcy laws, we went and picked up some equipment that a bankrupt restaurant had not paid for. Before all was said and done, the court ordered us to reimburse the cost for equipment we had sold but had never received payment for it!

The restaurant business is actually one of the riskiest businesses around, but it seems as if just about everybody wants to own one at some point in their life. Many people think that if they own a restaurant, they can just walk around the tables and greet their customers and make sure everyone is happy with their food and services. They don't realize that the owner is often the one bussing tables, washing dishes, or filling in for a cook who didn't show up.

People who succeed in the restaurant business work years to understand every facet of the business and know that they need adequate finances to support themselves until the restaurant becomes profitable, if it ever does. My son Robert tried it in Chapel Hill with a fast food health restaurant concept he had dreamed up for a project while in business school. It was a good idea, but the realities of finding dependable employees and steady customers in a college town were daunting. It took him about 18 months to realize the restaurant business was not his cup of tea.

This is why we focused much of our attention – and found much of our success – by going after state government contracts, which were typically put up for bid. That could result in large orders, but it was not easy work: there is a real art to bidding successfully – or maybe it's more of a science. Over several years, I studied the bid process carefully. I tried to identify the peculiar ways and whims of individual state procurement officers. I attended bid openings religiously: after bids were awarded, all of the bids were made public, so I would study my competitor's bids – especially the winning ones – calculating their percent markup on the merchandise and any particular strategies they had in presenting the bid. Winning a bid could sometimes come down to pennies on machines costing thousands of dollars. In this way I learned to prepare bids that could compete on price, service, and availability with other dealers across the state.

I was pleased to observe that the state's purchasing agents worked with a lot of integrity. They weren't looking for bribes under the table or any special treatment – they wouldn't even let you take them to lunch. The biggest thing they were interested in was learning to trust you and your business. They wanted to know that you really wanted to do business with the state, and that you could deliver what you promised. They kept records of how often they had problems with your equipment, and how good you were at servicing what you sold. We worked hard to ensure that we had a good reputation for service, and tried to satisfy the people who bought the machines any way we could. Sometimes we'd have to replace or repair a machine numerous times, and often do it even though the problem was due to the customer misusing the product. I can remember going into Central Prison in Raleigh myself to work on an icemaker that kept giving problems, even though I'm sure the inmates were mistreating it.

We were selling freezers and other refrigerated equipment before we knew anything about the technology of refrigeration. For repairs, we relied on a service man who was so temperamental that he drove me up the wall, and I told Pat we'd have to learn something about the subject to stay in the business. As we expanded our line, we also needed to learn more about refrigeration so we could talk intelligently with customers.

To deal with this, Pat and I took a course in refrigeration at Wake Tech, probably around 1981. This led us to pick up more refrigerated products like soft serve ice cream machines, walk-in coolers, and so forth.

We were selling a lot of equipment to keep things cool, but business would soon really heat up: I was about to find my passion.

CHAPTER **8**

I'm In Cells

H.T. Leary had been a classmate when I was finishing my undergraduate degree at Campbell, and he stopped by the showroom to see us one day around 1979. Like me, H.T. had an entrepreneurial streak. After working for ten years as a jail inspector for the state of North Carolina, he decided to quit inspecting jails and see if he could make more money selling products to them instead.

H.T. worked mostly along a swath from northern South Carolina, eastern North Carolina, and southern Virginia. He had only a dozen different items to offer his customers, and often sold them from the trunk of his car. Occasionally he would purchase kitchen equipment from us on credit, then resell it to jails. He was one of our slowest-paying customers, but he was a friend, and we didn't push him as hard as we did other delinquent accounts. We understood how difficult cash flow problems can be for small businesses.

The financial hurdles eventually became too difficult for H.T. to overcome, so after 18 months of trying to make a go of it, he had come by to tell us he was getting out of the business because he just didn't have the resources to make it profitable. He had decided to take a steadier job in a sheriff's office, and asked if we would be interested in buying his inventory.

I could see a lot of potential in sales to jails, so I asked H.T. not to make a move until I'd had time to think about whether we might want to expand our business in that direction and hire him to work for us. He agreed to wait, we both thought it over, and a short time later I purchased his inventory and brought him into the company.

Finding the key

Before going whole hog into the detention supply business, I wanted to study it carefully so we could maximize our chances of success. I knew that the key would be getting to know our customers and their needs, and there was much I needed to learn. I had worked with a lot of law enforcement people while serving as executive director of the Wake County Committee on Law and Justice back when I was mayor of Apex. Once, when we were short on police officers, I even rode around in a squad car to suggest the presence of law enforcement, but I'd never been inside a jail cell before.

I figured that learning the jail business was just a matter of time and effort. I had always been inventive and resourceful, and was confident that I could determine what jails needed, how to get it, and how to help them by marketing products they really wanted.

I started by pumping H.T. for information about how jails worked. After I felt confident that I knew which questions to ask, he and I headed up and down the east coast, interviewing every head jailer we could find. We would ask them what they needed to operate a safe and secure facility, and what kind of problems they faced most often.

I learned how inmates could make weapons or other contraband out of most everything imaginable, and how they hid things in their mattresses, other locations around the cell, or even in their own bodies. The most common and dangerous weapon they would come up with was a knife-like object called a shank. By rubbing and sharpening items against the edge of the bunk or in some other way, they could make sharp objects from toothbrushes, combs, razors, metal inserts in shoes, or dozens of other items. That suggested a need for products engineered so they couldn't be turned into weapons.

At that time, the two most visible competitors for the detention business were Walter Stephens in Ohio and Supreme Sales in Georgia. They both had small catalogs they would put out every year or two, with only limited items in them. Neither company was very aggressive, but they gave us ideas on how to market to jails. Putting two and two together, we learned the sort of supplies that jailers needed, and we saw that buying from a catalog worked well for them. We surmised that offering a wider selection of products, frequently updated catalogs, attractive prices, and dependable service would win us a lot of customers.

We were right.

Growing a catalog

Our first mailing couldn't rightly be called a catalog, but it got our name and a small selection of products before jailers in North Carolina and a few surrounding states. It was one legal sized sheet of light green paper printed front and back with black ink. It listed only a couple of dozen items, but we had them all in stock and knew we could deliver quickly. We didn't have a toll-free number at the time, so we just printed a message that customers could call us collect.

The response to the mailer was promising, so I immediately started planning a larger mailing. I still had the old headline machine from my days owning the newspaper and I knew how to cut and paste and lay out the pages for newsprint. Often I would cut the line art or pictures from the catalog of our suppliers and paste that into our publication. We started with a four-page version and ended up with an 8-10 page tabloid with red as an accent color.

The response to the first tabloid was predictably greater than our first mailer, and the phone began ringing a lot more frequently. I was beginning to believe we were on to something that could be really successful. I wanted to start mailing to every jail in the country, but Pat convinced me we should expand more gradually and try the Southeast first, to make sure we could handle the influx of orders. We managed to do that, and we began to add juvenile institutions, prisons, and mental health facilities to the list. I wouldn't be satisfied, though, until our list included the entire U.S.

We continued using the tabloid style for some time, but I soon came to believe that we needed a more professional looking bound catalog that could include more items. We didn't have the resources to hire a professional to do the catalog for us, so I began working at night on the floor of the showroom, laying out pages of items I thought jails needed. I included a number of items we didn't stock yet, and I didn't even know where to find them, but I figured we would cross that bridge when we came to it. I knew that jails would be interested in those products, and I wanted jailers to begin thinking of us as a reliable source for any product they might need.

> Phyllis Wickham: *When Bob was working on that catalog, he'd have pages spread all over the floor, and he would spend hours at this old headline machine that had a big dial on it. You'd dial the letter you wanted, then punch a button to make the letter. It was really labor-intensive, but Bob was committed to that catalog. He must have spent nearly a year on it, working late at night.*

The new publication turned out to be 185 pages, and it became too much for me to handle alone. Fortunately, we were able to contract with Bob Hall, a freelance graphic artist, to help clean it up and find us a printer.

Finally, though, the catalog was ready. We assembled a nation-wide mailing list and sent it out to potential customers with high hopes. We had bought extra stock and thought we were adequately prepared for the expected increase in sales, but the response overwhelmed us. The phone rang continuously for days, and it threw us into pandemonium. We only had five or six employees at the time, including Pat and me. Anyone who was near the phone would answer it, then go and try to pick the order. We didn't know how in the world we were going to fill those orders, especially for things we didn't actually have. We tried to explain our predicament to our customers and asked them to be patient with us, promising that we'd have the merchandise to them as soon as possible.

I had included cases of Colgate toothpaste in the catalog, for example, but the Colgate-Palmolive Company wouldn't sell to us wholesale because we were too small an operation for them to fool with. We searched all around and finally were able to order toothpaste in bulk from Baxter Hospital Supply, but the additional step between the manufacturer and us cut into our profit margin. In that and other areas, whether it was toothpaste from Colgate or replacement locks for cell doors from Folger Adams, we had to build the business before the major suppliers would sell to us. Today we are one of Colgate's largest distributors in the institutional field, but we don't rely on them entirely. We also sell house brand "Bob Barker" toothpaste, which we import from the Far East.

A surprising business booster

Ideally, one would never like to profit from a societal problem or human weakness, but we did: one of the main reasons we had struck gold in supplying detention centers was the growing drug culture of the 1970s and 1980s. The rapid influx of drug offenders led to big changes in the populations and policies of correctional institutions. There were two things going on: first, there was a large increase in the number of people being incarcerated. During the 1980s, for example, the prison population in the U.S. more than doubled, from 183,988 to 405,320 inmates. By 2000, the population was up to 621,149, with a high percentage of them in on drug-related charges. The customer base was consistently growing, and it was a captive audience.

Secondly, correctional institutions became responsible for providing both old and new inmates with more supplies. There was a day when jails and prisons furnished very little in the way of personal care items. If inmates wanted soap or a toothbrush, extra underwear or a deck of cards to pass the time, they had to rely on family members or friends to furnish the supplies. After drug use became so endemic, however, people would use those items as a way of smuggling contraband, including more drugs, into the correctional center.

As the problem increased, new regulations went into place, prohibiting visitors from bringing anything into the facility. That meant, of course, that jailers and prison officials had to begin providing all those personal items. Other correctional supply companies were slow to realize this, leaving jailers or purchasing agents scrambling to find the needed supplies from a variety of sources. With the research H.T. and I had done, I had a good idea of what detention officials needed, so I tried to position our company as a dependable one-stop shop for everything from hand soap to handcuffs, from clean socks to door locks, from tampons to toilets.

One of our big sellers was a selection of prepackaged individual "Admission Kits" containing basic hygiene items that could be given to inmates during the intake process. For jails, where many prisoners might be staying only a night or two, we had a simple kit with nothing more than a toothbrush, small tube of toothpaste, and a comb inside a plastic bag. Larger kits could include soap, razors, shave cream, deodorant, washcloths, and so forth. We developed some standard kits, but also allowed customers to customize their own kits by choosing from a list of items that we would pack for them.

When business started getting crazy and we got behind, we tried hiring some high school kids to pack the kits, and things got even crazier. We had a time trying to keep them on task and make sure they were doing it right.

As the orders continued to pile in, we added more regular employees to help answer the phones, pick the orders, and prepare them for shipping. That meant we also needed more people to order the merchandise, organize it in the stockroom, and ship it out. For several years, our sales grew by 30, 40, or 50 percent a year. In 1988 we grew by a ridiculous 82 percent. The seven employees we had in 1980 had grown to 21 by 1985 and 72 by 1990. We were still a small company, but a very busy one, and on our way up.

Growing pains

Cash flow is a constant problem for businesses such as ours, and it's exacerbated for small businesses that are growing rapidly. Here's the problem: we would order merchandise from our suppliers on an open account, and have 30 days to pay for it. But we might keep the merchandise in stock for 60 days before selling it – and then our customers could wait another 30 to 60 days to pay us. Even the state government, though dependable, is often slow in paying. So, even when things were going well and people were paying their bills, we had to pay our suppliers within 30 days of ordering our products, but were unlikely to see any income from the merchandise for 90 days.

We tried to get as many vendors as we could to extend payment terms from 30 to 60 days, but they were in the same boat we were in, and we had yet to establish enough credit for them to extend the terms very far without some payment. To cover that 60-day gap, you have to borrow money. You can have a vital, healthy, growing business but still have to borrow money. And, the more you grow, the more products you need to order, and the more you need to borrow. The same would be true when we later got into manufacturing: we had to borrow money to rent the space and buy the equipment and pay the workers long before we started realizing profits on what we made. Few companies ever get so far ahead that they can finance their own growth. In fact, economists know that a reasonable level of debt is a mark of a healthy business.

During those early years of expanding the business, I spent as much as half of my time trying to borrow money for what we needed to order, or to collect on merchandise we had shipped. We always offered a good discount to customers who paid quickly, but many were still slow to settle their accounts.

After a frustrating period of tramping to various banks to negotiate single loans, we were finally able to negotiate a $100,000 revolving line of credit at First Union Bank in Raleigh. Our loan officer was George Quick, one of the few African-American bank executives you ever saw in those days. George had a good understanding of our predicament. After we had shipped and billed an order to a customer, we would take the invoice to George. He would verify the transaction with the customer, then deposit money into our account as an advance. The customer would then send their payment directly to the bank, instead of to us.

This method worked well for a while, though it was rather embarrassing to me that our customers would pay the bank instead of us. Later on, it became quite a problem when we started using a factoring company to do the financing and customers were supposed to send the payment directly to us. Many of our customers had automated payment systems and were very slow about updating them. Even though we persistently reminded them to pay us directly, they'd continue to send our invoice payments to First Union. The bank was good about forwarding the checks on to us, but it still led to a delay in our receiving payment. It took two or three years to get all of our customers used to paying us instead of the bank.

Eventually, we grew large enough to attract the attention of multiple banks, and they started sending representatives to us, allowing us to negotiate for better rates and payment options.

Bulk mail and bulk sales

Although finances remained unsettled, we quickly realized that the catalog would continue to be crucial to our business. The national mailing list we'd worked hard to amass consisted of a box of perforated computer cards, ordered by zip code so we could take advantage of bulk rates when mailing, an important cost factor. One day Pat dropped the box of cards and some of them got mixed up. I don't remember how we got them sorted out again, but it didn't slow us down for long.

I had learned about bulk mailings and getting the lowest rates from the post office when I was in the newspaper business, but with a national mailing list, it could be quite complicated, so I hired an outside firm to do it. Soon after we started the bulk mailings, though, Pat decided we should try saving more money by sorting the finished mailer ourselves. Most all of our employees – maybe 10 people – sat around late one day to work on the project, but it soon became obvious even to Pat that sorting bulk mail was way too labor intensive for us to do by hand. We had to finish sorting that test mailing, but from then on we contracted with outside resources to sort the catalogs, affix the proper mailing labels, and get everything in proper order to obtain the greatest savings on postage.

Being consistent in putting out our sales catalogs was a key to our growth, and continues to be at the heart of our business. We noticed that our competitors only put out a catalog every couple of years, which wasn't nearly often enough to stay fresh. We wanted to keep our company visible to jailers and purchasing officers, as well as to introduce new products and adjust prices as needed, so we determined to provide more frequent catalogs. For a while, we went overboard and put out four catalogs per year. We discovered that our customers were becoming annoyed with the frequency of the catalogs, though, so we gladly cut back to two per year and saved money in the process.

The catalog served several functions then, as it does now. In addition to being our primary day-in and day-out sales tool, the catalog has also been the medium through which we introduced new products or changed prices on existing products. For several years during the 1990s, as we began to outsource and import more products, our prices actually went down more often than up, so having the latest catalog was important.

We learned that using the catalog in this way helps our customers as well as our company, as they can rely on the catalog for budgeting as well as ordering. A few hard lessons taught us to be consistent in that: sometimes we would take a hot new product to a trade show before it appeared in the catalog. When a customer who had seen it at the show called in to place an order, sometimes our sales staff wouldn't know anything about the product, the price, when it would be available, or even the item number to enter on the computer. That told us we had to do a better job of communicating within the company and training our sales staff on all new products, and that it worked most effectively to gear training and the receipt of inventory for the new product around our catalog cycle.

If you can't find it, make it

Aside from the headaches of finding financing, dealing with mailing issues, and discovering excellent employees, our biggest problem was finding suppliers who were reliable, economical, and committed to producing quality products. In some cases, we just couldn't find things that I knew correctional institutions would like to have. In other cases, shipments of merchandise we had ordered would be slow in arriving, or of poor quality.

This led me on a constant search for manufacturers or vendors who could supply the unique products our customers needed. At the time, our business was still so small that we could not demand the best prices or faster delivery times. I knew that, in time, we would need to begin manufacturing some of our own products in order to ensure the kind of prices, quality, and availability that we needed.

Early on, our greatest need was textile products: mattresses, sheets, blankets, towels, uniforms, and the like. I finally got up the nerve to buy a used commercial sewing machine, set it up on the second floor of the old hardware building, and started teaching myself to sew. I figured out how to make some of our products, and thought I could make some of them better. I knew that I could make them more cheaply, so I thought it would be feasible to begin making special size sheets, mattress covers, and blankets, among other things.

I found a lady named Doris Judd who had some sewing experience hemming pants legs for a dry cleaner. I hired her and put her to work making tear sheets: we'd buy a big roll of material that was finished on each side, then measure the length we wanted plus a little extra for a hem. After snipping a little cut at that point, we could easily tear the material straight across, sew a hem at both ends, and we'd have a sheet. Since prison bunks were only 25 inches wide, we could use fabric that was only 36 inches wide. Most sheets were 54 inches or wider, which I figured was just wasted fabric.

> Phyllis Wickham: *While we were still on Salem Street in Apex, Bob bought a sewing machine and when we couldn't find him, he would be upstairs in the dark, teaching himself how to sew. I will never forget one day when the phone rang and it was hard to understand what the person wanted, because we were already selling to something like 3,000 counties all over the country, and some accents were hard to make out. It turned out that Bob had been sewing sheets to take to a trade show, but we didn't know it. The woman on the phone wanted some green*

> *sheets like the ones she'd seen at the show, but we didn't have any more. We didn't know where the fabric came from, what color it was, what weight, or anything, so we had to talk her into something different. Bob was always working on a project that we didn't know about.*

In those days, jail mattress covers were made from PVC vinyl material that was very hot and hard to sleep on, so we developed a bag-like mattress cover from heavy cotton fabric that protected the mattress, extended its life, and made it more comfortable at the same time. That became a big seller.

We had been purchasing mattresses from a manufacturer in Salisbury, about 100 miles away. We had an old open-back truck that could carry about 100 mattresses if they were tied down properly. Almost every time we'd pick up a load to deliver to a customer, though, we'd lose one or two along the way.

The manufacturer in Salisbury mostly made regular home-type mattresses on a big sewing table with a mobile sewing machine that moved around the edge sewing the vinyl fabric together as if in a box. They used a cotton core treated with boric acid because it was fire-retardant, as required by prison rules. The basic design was insecure, however, because the sewing machine used only a single needle, and it was easy for inmates to open a seam and hide contraband inside the mattress.

The combination of inconvenient shipping and an inferior product led me to think we should start sewing our own mattresses. I went to the factory one day and watched very closely so I could see how they put the mattress together – then I set out to find a better way. I couldn't afford the kind of expensive sewing table that was typically used, but I knew we could make a better mattress that was also more secure, and do it more economically. After some experimenting, I devised a system whereby we would sew the two long sides and one short side of the vinyl mattress ticking inside out, using really strong thread. We'd then reverse the ticking, stuff the core inside, and use a double-needle sewing machine with the same strong thread to make a much more secure seam on the open end. It was incredibly difficult to get into our mattresses and hide contraband there, which made them popular with prison officials.

The process of turning the heavy vinyl cover inside out and then stuffing the padded core inside was easier said than done, though. Bob Fields, our fabric supplier, helped me design a wooden table with two long wooden planks sticking out that we'd use to squeeze the cotton pad flat so we could pull the mattress cover over it.

I wasn't crazy about the cotton core, though. It would get compacted and hard, for example, and some jails and prisons tended to use the mattresses so long that the vinyl would eventually crack, allowing moisture, sweat, or other body fluids to be absorbed by the cotton. When we started assembling our own mattresses, I ordered a heavier vinyl fabric that was still light enough to sew but nearly impossible to tear, impervious to water and also resistant to mold, mildew, and bacteria, as well as fire-retardant. To get around problems with the cotton core, I found another supplier who could make a firm polyester slab that wouldn't burn and was springy enough to prevent clumping or flattening.

Reversing the partially sewn cover was more complicated. It was physically laborious and especially hard on the hands. The women hated it. While visiting a textile show, I saw a guy who had developed a machine to turn blue jeans inside out, and I asked if he could design a similar machine that would work for our mattress covers. He built a contraption and brought it up, but it didn't work. Then he tried another design, and after we worked on it for a while and made lots of adjustments, we finally got it to do the job. The machine was basically a large tube: we'd pull the cover over the tube, then pump air from the tube to create a vacuum. The vacuum was strong enough to suck the cover inside of the tube, turning it inside out in the process.

This sort of can-do attitude and a belief that we can overcome any obstacle has been an underlying value of our company from the beginning. Even today, our six-point company "Code of Conduct" begins with "Can do approach in overcoming roadblocks to achieve commitments. There is always a way."

> Nancy Mills: *After the business picked up and we started making mattresses, it could get pretty crazy. There were just a few of us to answer the phones and pick the orders. There was no heat other than a wood stove out back that we had to stoke. There was a water fountain we couldn't use because it made a noise that made Pat go Loony Tunes. There was just one bathroom with a single commode, and we used the window in it to ship things out.*

> Phyllis Wickham: *We were on the first floor, but the ground outside was lower, so they would back a truck up below the bathroom window and we'd take all the mattresses we had made that day and throw them down into the truck. Part of my job was to make sure everybody used the bathroom before the truck showed up about four o'clock every day!*

There were so many regulations covering prison furnishings that we couldn't start selling the new product until it could be certified for use. To get it on the market, we agreed to supply 12 jails with the mattresses at no cost for a six-month trial period. They performed well and didn't exhibit any problems, so the state of North Carolina agreed to certify them. Soon we were shipping mattresses all over the country. Their clearly superior quality and competitive price made them an instant hit with our customers. For eight to ten years we were the only ones with that product, and mattress sales fueled much of our growth and profits during that time.

We were never ones to rest on our laurels, though, and have continued to improve the product. Today we use a special heating process to actually weld the seams together, making it even more difficult for inmates to get into it. We were able to get a patent on that process, as well as a model that has a built-in pillow. The mattresses need to breathe, and vents are a potential weak point, but we developed a hidden vent system that prisoners cannot find or exploit.

We discovered that some people still prefer cotton to the polyester core, believing it to be more comfortable.

Although most of our mattresses are made with polyester, we did a lot of research and added a line using a cotton core that's made from recycled blue jeans that have been shredded, treated with liquid boric acid, then formed and layered to produce a firmer product that maintains its shape. Other customers like foam mattresses, so after a process was developed to make the material suitably fire retardant, we added another line with a foam core.

Success with mattresses got our "cut and sew" department off and running, and soon we branched out into making prison uniforms and other products. We hired Phyllis Wickham to bring the supervisor experience we needed to grow that department, and she brought a more professional atmosphere to our unorganized method of manufacturing. As we expanded our space over the next few years, cut and sew operations grew to as many as 40-50 machine operators and occupied more than 40,000 square feet of floor space.

Businesses have to be nimble, though, and we are no exception. As market conditions changed, our cut and sew products could no longer compete with similar products manufactured overseas. We weren't happy about it, but to maintain competitive prices, we had to shut down much of our cut and sew operation in favor of outsourcing the job to overseas suppliers. We continue to make our own mattresses – up to 1,000 per day – along with a few other specialty items like shower curtains that we can make more effectively or economically than our suppliers.

> Phyllis Wickham – *I had come out of sewing infant wear and Bob wanted us to make jumpsuits and two piece suits in*

every size up to 10X. We now make up to 14 XL, if you can believe it. We once took a picture with three women in one jump-suit for the catalog. You never knew what kind of stuff Bob would buy. He'd find a deal on something and buy a bunch of it. When we'd complain, he would say "You can't sell from an empty wagon." One time he bought a whole bunch of fabric that turned everybody's hands blue. It was like working in a Smurf factory.

In the early years, finding sufficient and affordable fabric for our cut and sew operations was quite a challenge. North Carolina was still producing a lot of textiles at that time – there were big companies like DuPont, Cannon Mills, and Burlington Industries – but all the corporate offices were in New York City, so I had some traveling to do.

My first buying trip to New York was a zoo, as I tried to find company sales offices and then convince their sales reps to sell to a small-time manufacturer with no credit to speak of. I walked all over the city, trying to save cab fare, looking for fabric that was cheap enough to make a profit on when converted to clothing.

After several false starts, I finally connected with a young sales officer about my age who must have taken pity on me. He explained how I could buy overruns of fabric at good prices if I wasn't too choosy about colors. At that time, I couldn't afford to be choosy: we just needed the fabric.

He and I got to be friends, and he would call me from time to time when he had something at a really good price. As time went by, we developed a standard set of a half dozen colors like navy, green, blue, orange, and white. When they showed up in his inventory, he would save them for me. We mostly bought broadcloth, 6-8 ounces per square yard. Buying 15,000 to 20,000 yards at the time, we could usually get it for 70 to 80 cents per yard.

Later on, I discovered that Burlington Mills had a warehouse in Greensboro where they stocked all their seconds and overruns. The warehouse would have hundreds of rolls of fabric that they either had to sell cheap or destroy, so I would take a truck up there periodically and go all over the warehouse, looking through the overruns to see what fabrics we could use.

Those were hectic, incredibly busy years. Our business expanded almost exponentially and even though we were making use of four or five large buildings in downtown Apex, we were running out of space. We still had some serious growing to do, and if we were going to reach the next level, we would need more room.

And to find that space, we would have to move.

CHAPTER 9

Moving Up - and Out

Growing businesses can grow out of room about as quickly as children grow out of clothes. When it became apparent that we needed a better working environment than the four old buildings we were using on N. Main Street in Apex, we began inquiring about a suitable location. Our first thought was to acquire affordable land where we could build a new home for the business.

An Apex attempt

I was told about 36 acres of land on N.C. 55, just south of town. It belonged to the Cook family, and they were interested in selling, so I approached Woody Maynard, son-in-law of the property's original owner, to see if we could work something out.

The biggest issue with the land was that a railroad ran along the road in front of it. The upside is that the railroad's presence reduced the value of the land, making it more affordable. The downside is that we'd have to build a railroad crossing to get to it, and I had always found the railroad people hard to deal with.

When I was mayor of Apex, we had a problem with them because some of the railroad crossings were unsafe, but the railroad company would not even negotiate with us. They knew they had the advantage on us in most situations, so they made little effort to improve either the crossings or community relations.

I determined to use whatever leverage I had, though, and I knew there was a 35 mph speed limit for trains coming through town – and the trains were constantly violating it. I got their attention by having our chief of police notify them that the speed limit would be strictly enforced from then on. I had no idea how our police could have stopped a train, but the threat brought them around.

To pacify us and improve relations, the railroad company agreed to sell the town some rundown fertilizer buildings on several acres of land right on Main Street. They sold us the property for about a third of what it was worth, and agreed to lease us the old depot building for a dollar per year. The building was later renovated and served the town for some time as a rather unique public library. We took down the old warehouses and built a much-needed parking lot, and that helped to transform Main Street and kick off a long-running downtown revitalization.

Despite potential problems with the railroad, we pressed ahead with the land we wanted for expansion, and the Cook family heirs agreed to sell us the property for $7,000 per acre, or $250,000. I had no idea where I would get that amount of money, but I knew the family quite well and persuaded them to finance it for us at a reasonable rate of interest for 15 years.

After acquiring the land, the next hurdle was to get financing for a 50,000 sq. ft. building to go on it. At the time, we were banking with the Carolina Bank, which operated out of a mobile office in front of a shopping center. During our negotiations, the bank was purchased by BB&T, and the bank manager remained there. I continued talking to him about the loan, and he kept telling me that my request was before a bank loan committee at the main office in Raleigh. I later learned that he had not done the proper paperwork, and our request was never presented.

In researching building plans, we also ran into another problem. The land was outside the city limits, so there was no water and sewer running to the property. It was only 500 yards from the town's sewer treatment plant, however, and a county water line crossed the property's southern end, where a future thoroughfare had been planned – so I thought it would be a cinch to get water and sewer to the property. Engineers working on the project told me we'd need to build a pump station on the lowest part of the property to collect wastewater and pump it into the force main running beside the railroad to the treatment plant.

Unfortunately, the town had a policy that forbade pumping into the force main. I was no longer a member of the town board, and its new members would not even discuss it with me. I couldn't understand their disinterest in assisting someone who wanted to build a new industry in Apex – and they later regretted it when they saw our company grow into a 200-employee business with more than 500,000 sq. ft. of warehouse space, but in a neighboring town.

We decided to just hold onto the land in Apex and let it grow in value. Years later, when I was asked to lead a $30 million funding campaign for a new convocation center at Campbell University, we decided to sell the land and donate the proceeds to my alma mater. An investment group offered us $3 million for the land, with a million dollars down and the balance to be paid a year later. When the balance came due, they asked us to finance it for several years. We agreed to do so at seven percent interest, but they found a lower interest rate at a bank, borrowed the money, and paid us in full. I was really glad they did, because the company went into bankruptcy shortly afterward, in the real estate bust of 2008.

But back to our need for expansion: feeling exasperated with both the Apex town government and the banks, I began to consider other options for consolidating the business into an efficient space where employees could work in safe and adequate conditions.

A Fuquay-Varina solution

The solution came to me when I learned of an available building in Fuquay-Varina, a town about 10 miles south of Apex, on N.C. 55. Discovering the building was serendipitous: I had gone to Fuquay-Varina to see Don Lane, a dentist who had been recommended to me. I thought I just needed a filling, but he reworked my whole mouth. In the process, we became good friends and I'd often have lunch with him and his staff. Don was quite an entrepreneur. He had expanded his dental practice to 20 or 30 "Lane and Associates" dental offices scattered around eastern North Carolina, many of them featuring unusual architecture. He and I became business partners in some land investments, though he was bolder than I was when it came to investing in real estate.

When visiting Don's office one day, I noticed a large industrial property just off of Main Street that was for sale. I recalled having noticed the large building when I drove through Fuquay-Varina on my way to Campbell during my last year of college, and had always wondered what they made there.

I learned that the building was owned by a company called Cornell Dubilier, and it had been used for the manufacture of television antennas, the sort that used to decorate everyone's housetop before cable and satellite TV became the norm. The company had employed 600 people at its height, and had used helicopters to install twenty 30-ton air conditioners on the roof shortly before shuttering the building and moving its manufacturing operations to Taiwan.

The building, which faced E. Jones Street in downtown Fuquay-Varina, had 140,000 sq. ft. of space, with about 10-12,000 sq. ft. used for offices. I was immediately interested, but I had to call the realtor who was handling it three times before he would come down to show me the building. When he did, the electricity was off and it was impossible to explore the massive building with only a flashlight.

The owner wanted $2 million for the building and an adjacent parking lot. I thought that was too much, so I offered $500,000. He turned down the offer, so I set it aside and renewed my efforts to work out something on the Apex property.

About a month later, the owner had a change of heart and called me to say he was ready to negotiate on the property. I told him I'd have to see the inside of the building with the lights on so I could determine whether it would really work for us. He agreed to have the electricity turned on, and the facility was quite impressive. Pat and I began to dream about how we might utilize such a huge space.

After months of negotiation with the owner, we finally agreed on a purchase price that I thought was fair. Finding financing, however, was another matter. I went to every bank in town, and they all turned me down: no one believed we could pay for it because they could not understand our business of selling to jails and prisons. With no luck from the bank, I proposed to the seller that I would pay him $100,000 down if he would finance the balance for one year. He agreed. I don't remember how I came up with the $100,000, and I had no idea how I would find the remaining balance in a year, but Providence had intervened so many times before that I was confident we would come up with it somehow.

New name, new space, new growth

As our business transitioned and detention supplies became the focus of our marketing, we changed the name of the company from Bob Barker Equipment Company to the Bob Barker Company, adding "Inc." when we incorporated later on, in 1987.

Our move to Fuquay-Varina came a year earlier, in December of 1986. For a short while we had some operations going in both Apex and Fuquay-Varina, and barely had time to settle in to the new facility before hitting a major growth spurt: in 1987 we grew by 82 percent and the business grossed more than $3 million – and we became more attractive to bankers. We had begun banking with Raleigh Federal Savings Bank, a small bank that had branches in Fuquay-Varina, Apex, Raleigh, and a few other locations. Lib Rhew, a good friend who managed the Apex branch, believed in us and convinced bank executives to finance the remaining debt on the building for us.

After we worked that out, Raleigh Federal also began to open up and provided us with a larger line of credit so we could continue growing the business. In fact, George Sneed, the loan officer who worked with us, now sits on our board as an outside director. He was the first person we asked to do so.

With adequate space, we were able to expand in a number of ways. The building seemed so immense that we didn't even have to use pallet racks: we could just set pallets of boxes and products directly on the floor and pick from them there. It was a couple of years before we had to start building multi-level racks to conserve space.

> Robin Boraski – *In those early years, we didn't have many employees, and anyone who was available would pitch in and help pack orders. I remember that Bob would come back there like everyone else to pick and pack if he wasn't busy. He expected everybody to do that, and set the example. Bob didn't want anyone to get an answering machine when they called. In the early 1990s, the phone system would route to a sales person based on their area code, but if nobody answered, it would go back to the operator, who had to route it to somebody. They didn't want to have anybody*

> *on hold, so anybody with a phone was expected to take calls, if only to take a message and then pass it on to a sales person.*

With expanding business came the need for improved technology. We had been using an old TRS-80 computer from Radio Shack, but in 1987 we purchased a FACTS computer system to handle the inventory, billing, and accounting. We were also able to retire the old headline machine we'd been using and produce our catalog much more efficiently with desktop publishing software. In 1989, Ben Forbes, our chief accountant, built our first PC for basic needs such as producing documents and spreadsheets.

Our new catalogs were not only more attractive, but they included more products that we manufactured inhouse. With adequate space, we expanded our textile manufacturing until our cut and sew department occupied almost a third of the building, and it was soon joined by a metal fabrication unit.

> David Spivey – *Bob likes to try out every new product. One Sunday we were going to church and stopped at Harris Teeter for some groceries. My wife said "Look, there's a guy wearing boots with a suit!" It was Bob, on his way to church wearing a pair of our work boots. Sometimes he tests things to the detriment of his health – he tried a new razor once without bothering to use shave cream, and streaks of blood started running down his face.*

> Shannon Pilkington – *Soon after I started working at the company, I saw Bob. He was walking funny, so I asked him if something was wrong with his foot. It turned out that he was wearing two different shoes, trying them out. Another time I saw him scrubbing the floor with a toothbrush, like someone being punished. I wondered what in the world he was doing, but he was just testing the toothbrushes.*

We were selling a lot of steel bunks to jails, but we weren't happy with their quality. We had been purchasing them from Folger Adams, a large company that manufactured locks and other equipment. The bunks were shipped to us uncrated, and always seemed to arrive with damage that we would have to repair before we could resell them. I began looking around for a good welding shop in the area that could meet the same specifications, improve on the design, and make the bunks for us. This enabled us to conserve time, improve quality control, and prevent damage in shipment.

As time went by, we found that we could also get other steel products such as doors, tables, and lockers made for us locally. We soon had enough business to bring it all in-house and start our own metal manufacturing division in a 10,000 sq. ft. section of the building.

The business grew so well over the next few years that in 1992 we purchased an old 130,000 sq. ft. tobacco processing plant and moved our metal fabrication work there. Soon we were breaking, bending, and welding more than 100 different products for correctional facilities, all carefully designed to prevent them from being damaged or misused by inmates. We had a very innovative engineer, Todd Kruger, who could design almost any item I could dream up and describe to him, and together we created numerous new products that we thought prisons and jails could use.

One of our most successful collaborations based on customer input resulted in a "Van Cell," a modular cage designed to fit into standard 15-passenger vans. A head jailer had mentioned to H.T. Leary that he needed a more secure and efficient method for moving multiple prisoners. H.T. and Todd Kruger worked out a prototype and before long we had a product that enabled jailers to transport male, female, and youthful offenders in the same van, but in separate spaces. Over the past 20 years, we have continuously upgraded the product and have sold Van Cells in every state in the Union.

> Robert Danajka – *Bob was very heavily involved when we started manufacturing the mattresses, which we advertised as flame-retardant, so we had to test that. We were in a test lab doing what is called a "Michigan roll-up test" on an experimental mattress. To do the test, we'd roll up a mattress, stuff sheets inside, set it on fire, then go out and watch through a window. The mattress caught on fire so fast and made so much smoke that you couldn't even see the flames. Bob told me I should go in and check on it, but when I opened the door, a big glob of smoke came out. A few seconds later, the fire alarm*

came on, everyone evacuated, and the fire department came out. After that we didn't do any more Michigan roll up tests in the building.

Stephanie Driscoll – *The incident with the mattress test and the fire alarm didn't stop Bob from burning mattresses inside or outside either one. One day Ben Forbes and I we were getting ready to take an insurance person on a tour of the building and we caught a glimpse of Bob, who was out by the woods trying to set a mattress on fire. Ben said "You take him in the side door and I'll get rid of Bob." When Ben came back, he said "Don't even ask me what I had to do to get him away from here."*

Another day we were hosting a community tour and Bob was standing there with a blowtorch, trying to burn a mattress. You could find him in his office, holding something over his trashcan and trying to burn it with a little blowtorch. He believes in testing!

While we were making more products in-house, we knew that we had to be flexible and nimble enough to make changes with market conditions. I first travelled to Taiwan in 1983, and began some serious globe hopping in the late 1980s and early 1990s. My goal was to search the world for manufacturers who could provide us quality products and affordable prices. We had such success with this that there was a stretch in the 1990s when the prices we charged for many of our items went down rather than up.

We always prided ourselves on customer service and fast delivery of products, but as we grew a nationwide customer base, we were unable to ship to the entire country from Fuquay-Varina as quickly as we liked. That led us to explore the possibility of adding a warehouse on the West Coast. We started a search in 1990, and by 1991 we were serving West Coast customers from a leased warehouse in California. This enabled us to provide much faster service, and helped fuel growth to the point that we experienced our first month with a million dollars in sales.

> Debbie Paddack: *I'll never forget the first time we had a million dollar month. Bob was so excited that he paraded all of us up to the Golden Corral and bought us lunch.*

In 1993 we established a bid group to pursue large bids more competitively, and by 1994 we were able to leave the lease and purchase a warehouse in Dinubi, California. Sales continued to grow, and we celebrated our first two million dollar month.

From the very start of our business, our company has been known for innovation. We were never afraid to try new ideas or products. In 1993, we formed a group called the "Dream Team" to brainstorm new ideas and examine new ways of doing things. I suspect I was always the most irrational one on the team, throwing out any wild idea that came into my head. I got laughed at many times, but many of those ideas were either adopted or adapted by suggestions from other team members.

> Phyllis Wickham – *Bob would come up with some hysterical ideas for new products. Starting the Dream Team helped to manage his creativity, putting more minds into the process.*

> Nancy Mills – *We had to come up with something called the "J Process." Bob would tell everyone that if they needed something, we would find it or make it, so sometimes we ended up with some really non-standard stuff. It complicated the inventory system, so I started assigning a "J" number code ("J" for "junk") to all these odd items, or partial amounts because Bob would sell 20 items out of a 144 count box and leave us to figure out what to do with the rest. There was no profit in it, but Bob was the boss.*

> Trish Powell – *Whenever a customer wanted a product we didn't have, Bob would always promise that we could get it or make it. He'd then give them my business card and say "Trish will get it for you." ... I am the highest person on the "J List" to this day because I go get everything the customer asks for.*

The Dream Team met each week to discuss and make decisions about what new products we wanted to pursue – and we were always looking for something new, never content to stick with the status quo.

Successful businesses know how to innovate, but also how to manage their product offerings sensibly. So, along with the Dream Team, we established a "Nightmare Team" whose job was to analyze our sales figures and identify products that weren't selling so we could weed out unprofitable items. This was hard for me, because they'd bring me a list of products to drop, and I hated to let products go. Sometimes we'd have considerable inventory of something that wasn't selling, and they'd want to just throw it away to make room for something else. I was always asking if we could find a way to combine it with another product so it would move. Sometimes I'd find something they'd thrown into the dumpster, and I'd take it back out, certain that we could find a way to repackage it and sell it. We later started a "Bob's Bargain Basement" section of the catalog to help move merchandise that we needed to clear out.

> Phyllis Wickham – *I once went to a trade show with Bob in Florida. We had these new "heater meals" (like the military's MREs, or "Meals Ready to Eat"). They were packaged meals that would keep forever, and had a built in heating unit. Bob thought we could get jails and prisons to stock up on those so they'd have them in a crisis situation, or if there was a power outage, or whatever. He would sit on a metal table that we manufac-*

> *tured and eat them as people walked by. He was convinced we could sell it.*
>
> Melane Faucette – *We did sell a lot of them, but we finally discontinued them after they didn't move as well as Bob had hoped: then we had to eat the remaining stock.*

Some of our dream ideas worked out quite well, and when others did not, we learned to be willing to let them go. For example, in 1995 we decided to expand our marketing to nursing homes and extended care facilities. We produced the first of three catalogs tailored just for that market, but it did not prove to be profitable, and after a few years we dropped the effort.

Another time, we ordered a big lot of black socks, thinking prison officers would buy them for use with their uniforms. We weren't selling other products to officers, however, so the socks didn't move. There was nothing wrong with the product, but it was the wrong time and the wrong marketing approach. Years later we created a special section of the catalog with equipment and clothing for law enforcement and prison officers. We called it "For Officers Only" and put it in the back of the catalog, but turned the pages upside down with the back cover designed so you could flip it over and it looked like a completely different catalog.

> David Sears – *Bob always hated to throw anything away. When I was distribution manager, we were doing some cleaning up at the Purfoy building, and*

Sheila Staton brought me some really dirty bedsheets she had found. They looked like they'd fallen to the floor and been run over by the forklift. I told her to throw them away. About two hours later, Bob came walking down the hall carrying those sheets – he'd just happened to come by as they were emptying the dumpsters, and he'd seen them. He asked me what the sheets were doing in the dumpster. When I explained that they were too dirty to sell, he said "You have a washing machine back in manufacturing, don't you? You can iron them, can't you?" We learned to clean and repackage things when we could, rather than throwing them away. But Bob loved a good deal and would sometimes buy stuff we couldn't sell. He'd come back from China and say he'd bought a few things – and it would be whole containers of shoes.

Shelia Staton – *I'll never forget when Bob bought a whole shipping container of purple tennis shoes: sized 14, 15, and 16. They were so big we called them clown shoes. I don't know if we ever sold any of them. That man loves a bargain.*

Neil McCraney – *We had a whole bunch of shoes once that got mildewed because the shipping container leaked. It took a*

> *long time to convince him to let us throw those things away. Bob was also a stickler about wanting every shipment that came in processed and put on the shelves that day, but sometimes we just couldn't do it. Bob would come by early in his tracksuit while getting his morning exercise, and he would always check to see if we had put up everything that came in the day before. Eventually, we learned how to hide stuff in the corner.*

After that killer year in 1987, we continued to expand, though at a more measured pace. Our son Robert joined the company as our first director for strategic planning, and led us in a planning retreat in 1996. That same year we experienced our first month of three million dollars in sales, so we certainly needed to be thinking strategically.

From the time we published our first catalog, we had largely depended on catalog sales. H. T. Leary, who had helped introduce us to the jail and prison business when he joined the company, was our only outside sales person. In 1997, however, we expanded our outside sales force to five.

I had thought we would never run out of room in that 140,000 sq. ft. building on E. Jones Street, but even with the purchase of a separate building for the metal fabrication unit, we began to feel cramped. More importantly, the building itself had not been designed for our needs: the ceiling was only 16 feet high, which limited the number of pallet racks we could stack. The building was also constructed on two levels, which was not conducive to picking orders. Only about 60,000 sq. ft. was available for distribution purposes.

We decided on a strategy of building a new facility designed to help us receive products, store them, pick them from the pallet racks, and ship them as efficiently as possible, with various levels of automation built in. We purchased land on Purfoy Road, on the southern edge of Fuquay-Varina, and completed a 200,000 sq. ft. facility in 1998. Our daughter Nancy was in charge of that project, and successfully guided it to completion.

The new building was designed with wide aisles and 35 ft. ceilings, which allowed us to install five level pallet racks that could be equipped with an automated lift system: an employee stands on the lift, and a computer guides it to the location of each needed product so the stock picker can grab the needed items. This enabled them to work far more efficiently than if they had to guide the lift and find the products on their own. With its five-level pallet racks, hi-tech picking system, an efficient shipping process, speedy forklifts, and quality employees, the new addition quickly proved its worth.

One of the reasons we have been so successful is that we listen to our customers. They know where their problem areas are, and have often suggested ideas for a product we could make that would address their needs. For example, jail and prison officials are always concerned about inmates hiding contraband in their cells. We developed mattresses with a tough vinyl cover that has no visible seams, and even the vents are invisible, so inmates can't find and access a weak spot. For those who want to be even more careful, we offer shampoo and other toiletries – even bars of soap – that are see-through, making it difficult to hide contraband in them.

Some of our best innovations have been in shoes. For everyday use, prison officials prefer that inmates have shoes without laces – which can be turned into weapons or used to commit suicide – so some sort of step-ins have become the norm. For years, canvas shoes were standard, but the inner soles came out when they were washed, causing a problem if they got mixed up with other shoes. We designed a shoe with a sewn-in inner sole, but the canvas shoes are still subject to wear and coming apart.

One of our most recent innovations combines the best of a standard step-in with the convenience and popularity of plastic clogs: we designed a bright orange shoe made from comfortable and durable Ethyl Vinyl Acetate (EVA) material that is also antimicrobial, odor-resistant, and waterproof. The one-piece shoe is exceedingly hard to tear or damage, and has a non-slip tread that provides good traction in all conditions. We're anticipating that it will be a big seller.

People outside of the detention industry sometimes approach us with ideas, too. I've had people from all walks of life approach me about making a product that they thought up and believed it would serve our customers. Only a few of those have turned out to be useful ideas, but I have always given people the respect of an audience and listen to what they have designed or dreamed up.

New problems

Businesses are always happy to see growth, but successful business leaders learn to anticipate that growth will bring with it the potential for problems. Some problems you can predict and plan for, but others may spring up unexpectedly, and they have the potential to knock your company's health right off the tracks.

Early on, we had some issues with accounting. We were doing a good job of keeping up with who owed money to us, but we did not have an effective system of tracking to whom we owed money. That made our own accounting system ineffective, and didn't help us any with banks, who want to have an accurate idea of your debts as well as your receivables. That problem could have been predicted, but at one point our growth outstripped our accounting, and we had to really play catch-up for a while.

Perhaps the biggest threat to our business came in the form of an unfortunate software purchase. In the late 1990s, we had outgrown the software we used for billing, shipping, tracking inventory, and other needs. Nancy Mills was our chief operating officer at the time, and she pushed hard for us to find a new system. My son Robert had come to work with us, and was heading the Information Technology department. This was a time when a number of companies were beginning to market what was called ERP (Enterprise Resource Planning) software. SAP and Oracle were the biggest players in the field, but we weren't a major company, and the price was daunting.

After surveying available software systems, Robert settled on a system promoted by JD Edwards, a highly respected company, but smaller and newer to the field of software management tools. The software promised to do everything we needed, and was called "One World." Soon, however, we realized that we had entered a "Lost World."

Despite JD Edwards' past reputation, they were marketing the software long before it was ready for prime time, misrepresenting it as being capable of running day-to-day operations out of the box. Today we often speak of software in the final stages of development as a "beta" version. Unfortunately, the software we bought was hardly an "alpha" version: it was filled with bugs and unfulfilled promises.

Basically, we were a little too anxious to go with the latest computer platform as well as software, and as Robert put it, "we went from the leading edge to the bleeding edge." We didn't test the software enough to discover all the core problems and challenges with it, and made the mistake of believing sales officers who promised that the company would faithfully fix problems as they emerged. We phased in the new software at the same time we were setting up the automated system in the new distribution center, so we were completely dependent on it – and when it proved unreliable, it threw the whole company off.

As we tried to get the system running, we trusted the software company too much, and didn't give adequate attention to our employees, some of whom were pointing to serious problems with the program. The software was supposed to manage inventory and the picking and shipping of orders, but it was incredibly inconsistent. We couldn't keep up with inventory, find things in the warehouse, or accurately track shipping. Some orders would be filled multiple times, others not at all. Instead of shipping within 24 hours, as we usually did, orders were taking days to fill.

Similarly, the program failed us on the accounting side. We didn't know who owed us money or how much. It was a nightmare for our employees, and frustrating for our customers. Our reputation was in danger of going down the tubes, and if we hadn't had so many dedicated employees who were willing to work late into the night trying to sort through the problems, figure things out, and ship orders by hand, we could have been set back for years.

After six to eight months of working with JD Edwards and failing to ever get the software in working order, we hired a consultant to help us transition to another product. We ended up going with supply chain software from a company called Apprise, and it worked very well for us.

While that was a major headache for us, we just didn't contemplate that a company with a great reputation could put out such a sorry product. We entered a lawsuit against JD Edwards, went to arbitration, and managed to recover most of what we had spent to purchase the software, but the damage to our reputation was something we had to repair on our own. We weren't the only company to fall victim to the "One World" fiasco. JD Edwards struggled after that, and the company was purchased by Oracle.

The lesson was a hard one for us, but we learned from it, and pressed ahead.

We had to learn and adapt in other ways, too. As we grew through our own host of internal changes, we worked within an economic system that was rapidly becoming a global marketplace, and we had to adapt to that, too.

It's a good thing I like to travel.

CHAPTER **10**

Frequent Flyer

Our business was taking off in the 1980s, but I knew better than to think we could rest on our laurels and assume that market conditions would allow us to always do things the same way. There was always pressure to keep prices as low as possible and to gain whatever edge we could over our competitors.

I had a sense that imports would have to be an important part of our product mix, so I set out to explore options as early as 1982, with a trip to Taiwan. Fortunately, I enjoy traveling, even to prisons! I may have been in more jails than anybody, visiting customers in jails and detention facilities in almost every state. But business ventures have also taken me to nearly every U.S. possession overseas, as well as nearly 100 countries around the globe.

Most of my overseas travel has been in search of quality affordable products to satisfy our loyal customers. There was a time when products branded with "Made in Japan," "Made in Taiwan," or "Made in China" were the butt of jokes because of their poor quality. As the 1970s progressed, however, Japanese automakers and electronics manufacturers proved that they could make quality, desirable products, and that was just the beginning of a growth curve in the quality and quantity of products coming from Asian countries.

Go East, young man...

My first trip to Asia was to Taiwan, and on the way there I also made a brief foray into Mainland China. The country was still a long way from the heated manufacturing growth that developed as the country began to embrace a modified form of capitalism. At the time, most of the country remained off-limits to outsiders and most of the people were still living in communes. It was the most backward-looking place I had ever been.

We left Hong Kong on a bus that ventured into the Guangdong province of southern China. Security was very strict: an armed soldier rode on the bus with us to make sure we were not making unwanted contacts or spying on their country. We were allowed to see only what they wanted us to see. The Guangdong countryside was very rural at the time, but today there are major cities populated with shining, modern skyscrapers. I saw incredible changes in 25 years, and the changing landscape is more amazing each time I return.

My original intention in going to Taiwan was to look for a provider who could make clothing suitable for correctional facilities. I met with a lady there who claimed that she knew all the clothing factories, and could take me to visit them. I had little choice but to trust her, so we set out on an expedition to visit manufacturers, many of which were on the other side of the island. To get there, we traveled by bus over the mountains and nearly all the way across the island. The crowded bus trip took half a day, and I felt very uncomfortable with about a hundred eyes staring at me the whole trip. I realized, though, that visitors from the West were probably quite rare. The Chinese passengers on the bus must have been very curious, because they watched every move I made.

The trip back was easier: when the long day drew to an end, my guide hired a taxi for the return trip. It was late in the night when I got back to the hotel, and I was happy to be there.

I thought the day was profitable, though, as we found several manufacturers that I thought could work for us. I placed an order with one of them for about $20,000 in the form of a bank letter of credit held by the woman who was acting as a broker for us. The letter of credit serves as a negotiable instrument: when the vendor delivers the ordered goods (or something that might pass for them) to the shipping company, the seller receives a bill of lading, which can be exchanged for cash or an account deposit at almost any bank.

I knew nothing about the woman who was representing me, other than she had an office claiming to be an exporter. The letter of credit I made out to her was good for sixty days. If the vendor failed to ship the order within that time, it would expire.

After returning to the U.S., I made frequent attempts to contact the woman and get a report on how things were going with our order, but to no avail. I began to be concerned that she might put any kind of junk in a crate, call it clothing, and ship it in order to collect my $20,000.

I was greatly relieved when 60 days had passed and the letter finally expired. I didn't have the goods I wanted, but at least my money was safe. This was a learning experience for me: not everyone can deliver what is promised. Fortunately, we have had only one other experience like this in more than thirty years, involving hundreds of international orders.

While in Taiwan, I was so amazed by the cheap garment prices that I bought five suitcases and filled them with clothing for my wife, Pat, and our children, Nancy and Robert. The problem was, I did not know how I was going to get everything back without paying large fees to the airline for the extra luggage. When I arrived at the airport, there were all kinds of porters wanting to help me, so I promised one of them ten dollars if he could get my luggage checked without any extra charges. Ten U.S. bucks was a lot of money to them at that time, and he managed to make it happen.

Another lesson from that trip involved keeping up with the value of local currency. I hired a cab to take me from the airport in Hong Kong to my hotel, and when we arrived the driver said my fare was $20. I thought the price seemed awfully high, but I pulled out a $20 bill and paid him. After checking into the hotel, I realized that the cab driver had quoted the price in Hong Kong dollars, which would have been about $2.50 U.S. The cabbie was only too happy to keep my American twenty, while I kicked myself and chalked it up as another learning experience. I couldn't afford many more lessons like that.

I have found most business people to be honest and trustworthy. Whether they are Chinese, Indian, or Brazilian, they usually want the same things any businessperson does: a relationship that can be profitable and good for both parties. When we started doing business with the Chinese, they were not very savvy in business, but they were so anxious to do business with the Americans that they would often promise more than they could deliver. Much of this, I think, resulted from misunderstandings related to language and culture.

My experience was that the Chinese have a great sense of humor. The people I dealt with would laugh frequently at my poor attempts at joking. I found that I could get better prices by making a ridiculously low offer and then cracking a big smile. They always teased me by saying that Americans always want cheap, cheap prices.

That trip to China was the first of many and the beginning of a positive and profitable relationship. Today, our company has a full-time office in Shanghai staffed with Chinese employees who find sources for the products we need, check quality at each factory we deal with, and handle shipping. Having a local presence has been a major help in finding quality vendors, not only in China, but in other parts of the East, including India. Chinese employees have helped us overcome language and cultural differences, which puts us on a more even footing with possible suppliers. We treat our Chinese employees with the same respect that we do our employees here in the states, and they are very appreciative.

> Maria Elena Gomez – *I went to India with Bob and he was really careful about eating locally prepared food for fear he would get sick – so he ate only salads, and then got sick from eating all those uncooked vegetables washed in dirty water. At one place, there were a lot of beggars, and Bob started giving away money. That was very scary*

because people started mobbing us, but we managed to get away OK. Bob is always willing to explore the local culture. We went to Puerto Rico for a convention and he ate everything there. He liked going out and connecting with local people and trying the local food. Bob drove all the time like he knew the place. It was amazing. He was driving faster than everybody else. The police there keep their lights flashing all the time, and I often thought they were coming after us.

NAFTA points south...

There was a time when our cut and sew operation had as many as 50 employees, and we made a lot of our own uniforms, bedding, and other textile products. As market conditions changed, however, much of the textile industry moved offshore, and we had to follow it there if we wanted to remain competitive. After the North American Free Trade Agreement (NAFTA) went into effect in 1994, we began looking at Mexico as a potential source of textile products.

On my first trip to Mexico, my teenage son Robert accompanied me. He was taking Spanish in high school and asked to come along, promising that he could interpret for me. After arriving, we discovered that very few of the business people we met could speak English. And, to our sorrow, we also learned that Robert could not understand their Spanish.

With our inability to communicate, that first trip was not very successful. To top it off, we had gotten into Mexico without having our passport stamped and that created a big problem when we started to leave. Immigration officials took us into a small room to question us as to how we got into Mexico without coming through customs and passport control. Unfortunately, we didn't know. I think we just walked right by the passport and customs desks without realizing that we needed to go through the lines. I thought for a while they were going to lock us up until we could prove that we were not smugglers, but we were finally released – after having learned yet another travel lesson.

I made a number of trips to Central and South America looking for good sources of fabric, blankets, and underwear. My first trip to Central America was to Guatemala, and this time my daughter Nancy came along. She and another student had started a small import clothing business while in college, and she was looking for unique, colorful garments that would appeal to the younger crowd she was targeting at music festivals, surf shops, and small boutiques.

The trip was not overly successful, but we enjoyed the beautiful country as well as the kind and loving people. I returned to Central America a short time later, traveling to Honduras and El Salvador. I was able to start doing business with a clothing manufacturer in El Salvador, but it was not very satisfactory. It was a small operation, and not able to deliver on a consistent basis.

I needed some help, and I found it in Flavio Ferreira, a Brazilian native who started traveling with me. Flavio's language skills helped us tremendously, because he spoke both Portuguese and Spanish.

Flavio's arrival was really serendipitous. When I ran the weekly newspaper in Apex, a Brazilian lady named Jo Woodie worked with us for a while, but she and her

American husband later decided to live in Brazil. After the move, she called me one day to say she had become good friends with a talented young couple there who wanted to come and study in America.

The young friends were Flavio and his wife, Zina. Knowing our hospitable nature, Jo asked if Flavio and Zina could possibly live with us for about six weeks, until they got acclimated to the country and found a place to settle in. We were happy to host them, and they turned out to be delightful people who soon became like family. Flavio and Zina had just married in Brazil before leaving, but they wanted to get married again in the U.S. to be sure it was official here. We talked with our pastor and arranged to have the wedding at our church. Woodhaven Baptist was a new church start that we had helped to begin just a few years before, and theirs was the first wedding held there.

Zina had been born in the U.S. during a short period when her parents lived here, so she was a citizen, and she spoke perfect English. Flavio's English was more limited, but he enrolled in our community college and picked it up really fast.

We hired both Flavio and Zina to work with us for a while. Zina earned a degree in computers while working for us, and later took a great job with IBM. Flavio was a hard worker who rose through the ranks in our company. As he and I traveled all over the world in search of affordable, quality products, he became a supervisor in sourcing for our company.

After about ten successful years in the states, Flavio and Zina returned to Brazil. Today Flavio is managing a 600-employee meat packing plant that specializes in beef jerky and ships most of its products to the U.S. We have been able to visit them a couple of times, and they are great hosts. It gives us joy to know we had a role in contributing to their success.

Trade missions

Around 1990, I had the honor of joining about a dozen business people from North Carolina on a trade mission to Russia, just as the country began opening up to the outside world. We flew to Finland for a one-night stopover, and then on to Moscow. There we were met by a large group of would-be entrepreneurs who were ready to try capitalism after almost a century of communism. They were very eager to learn everything we could teach them about business, and we were eager to teach them. They listened intently to every thing we said, even though it had to be translated for them. They held several receptions for us, and I remember that they drank a lot of vodka while toasting just about everybody and everything.

I had gone there to see if we could contract business both ways, buying and selling. They were mainly interested in buying American goods for resale, but there was a problem: they had no money. They wanted us to ship to them on consignment, on the promise of future payment. Our group showed little interest in this type of trade, so we did not accomplish as much as I'd hoped.

During one trade show, though, they really captured my attention with a number of spy devices the KGB – the Russian security agency – was trying to sell. One of the devices enabled the user to see around corners without being seen, and there were quite a few electronic devices used by their military.

CHAPTER 10

As the year 2000 rolled around, I was invited to join another trade mission, this time to China. We had a Chinese employee, Winnie Tan, who set up a visit to Dalian, her hometown. Dalian is on the northeastern coast of Korea Bay, a clean and beautiful city that looked very European.

Dalian was not originally a Chinese city: Japanese and Russian invaders settled it near the end of the 1800s, wanting to establish a colonial city there. A group of Russian architects who were fascinated with French culture designed the city with elegant Parisian-inspired squares studded with artistic sculptures, lush lawns and western-style fountains. These formed the architectural basis of the present city, radiating outward from central squares. Today, stylish women troopers patrolling the square have become a feature of the city.

Our host in Dalian was an eccentric multi-millionaire who was building a five star hotel there. He was determined to impress us and treat us well, and when his hotel was not finished in time, he paid for us to stay in another five star hotel.

We took North Carolina's Secretary of State Elaine Marshall with us on the trip, along with Pamela Davison, the director of the World Trade Center in Raleigh, N.C., and my good friend Wally Brooks. It was quite an experience: we were wined and dined like celebrities, driven around in limos, and interviewed for TV every time we stepped out of the car.

The mayor of Dalian, Bo Xilai, invited us to a large dinner with all his vice-mayors. He invited us to his office, which overlooked a large park. From his personal balcony, he could control the classical music being played in the park. Bo was much more outgoing than most Chinese, an easy man to like. He went on to serve as governor of Liaoning Province, and from 2004 to 2007 served as the minister of Commerce. In 2007 he was appointed as the Communist Party secretary for Chongqing, a major southern city. Quite a rising star, Bo was once rumored to be in line to become premier, but politics led to his downfall in March of 2012. The last I heard about him, he was under house arrest.

After our sojourn in Dalian, we went to Beijing for some sightseeing and our host provided a young lady named Dandan Liu to be our escort and interpreter. Dandan, who allowed us to call her Anna, was in her twenties and married to a young engineer named Zhili Wang. She taught at a small college and was delightful to be with. Anna was an excellent guide and knew the city well, along with local culture and history. She invited us to speak to her class on entrepreneurship, and I found her students to be fascinated about how business was done in the U.S. They must have asked a hundred questions.

In the three days we were there, we became fast friends with Anna and her husband, and when she expressed a desire to study in the U.S., I promised to help all I could. She was able to get a student visa and scholarship at Temple University in Philadelphia, where she earned masters and doctoral degrees in mass communication. Her husband came later, attended Stevens Institute of Technology in New Jersey, and obtained a masters degree in construction management. After graduation, they moved to North Carolina where she is now a professor at the University of North Carolina at Pembroke, and he is an environmental engineer with a firm in Charlotte.

They are the parents of two beautiful children, a girl and boy, and have also become part of our extended family.

Trade Shows

Not all of our traveling is overseas, of course. Our sales people and account managers go and visit customers, and we always have a good representation at trade shows like the American Jailer's Association (AJA), which is the biggest of them, the American Corrections Association, and a variety of meetings for sheriffs and other corrections officials.

Trade shows offer a good opportunity to give employees a treat while also exposing them to more aspects of our business, so I like to take different people with me to the shows, teach them some tricks of the trade, and to treat them well while we are there – except when playing a little joke, of course.

> Neena Mann – *I was at one show when we had just brought out the little short-handled toothbrushes. Bob would throw them at people to get their attention and then point at me.*

> Pam Whitmill – *We always have some sort of promotional giveaways at the booth. After a while I had to plead with the people in marketing not to use balls or Frisbees, because Bob would throw them at people to get them to come over.*

Building a business is all about relationships, and you especially have to relate well to your customers. When we're at a trade show, 95 percent of the people who stop by will just say "We buy all our stuff from you" and then move on. But if they move on, we can't sell them any new stuff, so I would always stop them and ask "Are we taking good care of you?" That would often begin a conversation so that we could show them some of our new products and hopefully sell them more.

> Tammy Norton – *Bob really tries to stay in tune with our customers. He has a gift of talking with our customers at any level. We've all really learned from him about how to do a better job of interfacing with our customers. Not long after I became an account manager, I was with Bob at the AJA, which was in Columbus, Ohio that year. Columbus is in Franklin Co., and the sheriff there, Sheriff Karnes, was a big, intimidating man. He was in my territory, and Bob told me I should go introduce myself to him and tell him he'd done a fine job helping to host the show. I was scared, but I went up to Sheriff Karnes and introduced myself and we talked about the Bob Barker Company, and I soon got over my fear. Through the years, Sheriff Karnes and I became good friends. That experience taught me that I could walk right up and develop relationships with people. Bob taught me that.*

One year I took several people with me to China for the Canton Trade Fair, one of the largest trade fairs in the world. We were more interested in buying than in selling, so I'd divide us into teams and we'd go looking for potential vendors who could manufacture or supply the products we wanted with good quality at good prices, and also to look for new products.

Everybody we'd talk to would hand us a business card and a catalog, and before long you'd be carrying around a whole stack of material. I was glad Mark Gaines had brought a backpack, because every now and then I'd pass what I'd collected on to him.

> Mark Gaines – *I wish I hadn't taken that backpack. By the end of the day Bob would have given me 20 or 30 pounds of catalogs and stuff to put in it. After we'd been there several days, I had a stack of catalogs in my room more than two feet high – and left most of it there. One day toward the end of the show, Mike Reed, Bob, and I decided to walk over to the section where they were promoting outdoor recreation supplies. It didn't take long before Mike and I lost track of Bob. We looked and looked, and finally found him on the floor, stretched out on a camp mattress. He liked it so well that he was about to tell Mike to call back to the states and get the finance department to approve purchasing two container loads of those mattresses. It was all we could do to talk Bob out of that. We later made some mattresses that were very similar.*

I love to travel, and believe it should be fun, and I like to share that with the employees who go with me. One year we were in Oklahoma, so I took the crew to a different steak house every night. Even though we were in steak houses, though, Neena Mann wanted to order chicken, and I enjoyed giving her a hard time about it. Neena also gave us quite a ride one year. She started working for us at a young age, and when we collected our rental car at the airport, I told her she could drive. When we got to the highway, a line of sheriff's cars came by, all going to the same convention. They were flying, and Neena just settled into the convoy and sped along with them.

Watching people like Neena grow and develop in the company has been special. We've enjoyed business most when it's not just about business. In various ways, the Bob Barker Company has always been a family affair.

CHAPTER **11**

Transitions: a Family Affair

One of the best things about the Bob Barker Company, I believe, is our strong, family-oriented approach. I grew up doing all kinds of odd jobs along with my brothers. When I started this business in 1972, my brother Jack was working with me as we started selling slush machines to convenience stores and food operations. After a couple of years, Jack went back to running a grocery store in Dallas, N.C., but almost 15 years later he came back to work with us, in sales.

My two sisters, Pauline and Shelby, also worked with the company, filling various jobs until their retirement several years ago. Pauline, the oldest in the family, was especially stalwart, not fully retiring until age 84.

Jack was not the only brother who helped sell our products. My older brother Clarence worked as a salesperson covering a number of states around Tennessee, where he lived. Clarence's son Jeff, who is blind, is also a talented musician. He sometimes traveled with Clarence to state jailers' conventions and entertained them on keyboard or piano.

Closer to home, my wife Pat built on her masters degree in chemistry from Duke while developing hypoallergenic products for the Almay cosmetics company, and her Almay paycheck went a long way toward getting the earliest incarnation of the company off the ground. Her greatest contribution, however, began in 1977 when she left Almay to work full-time with what was then called Bob Barker Equipment Company. As I've said before, Pat's analytical and conservative thinking probably kept us from going bankrupt several times by pulling me back from some crazy ideas. She has proven invaluable to the business throughout her career.

Our company has always maintained a relatively flat structure. While I held the title of President and Pat was officially Executive Vice President, we worked so closely together that most of our managers reported to both of us. That may sound a bit iffy, but people adapted well to our rather loosely defined dual roles. For example, they learned that for any major initiative, they had to sell me on the vision – but they had to be prepared to show Pat the return on our investment.

Our children, Nancy and Robert, began working at the company while they were still in elementary school. At first they did odd jobs like dusting products in the showroom or carrying out trash. As we got more and more involved in supplying detention facilities, they helped put personal hygiene kits together.

Robert was growing up as personal computers were first coming on the market, and he was a whiz with technology. In the late 1970s, when he was in the fourth grade, Robert actually helped us to select the first computer we purchased for the company.

Our daughter Nancy had an artsy bent through high school, so we were surprised when she decided to study business when she enrolled at the University of North Carolina-Wilmington (UNC-W). She did well, graduating cum laude with a recommendation from her logistics professor to study for a masters in business.

Nancy

We did not assume that our children would build their careers with us and never pressured them to do so, but we were happy when they chose to join the company. When Nancy graduated in May of 1991, she first looked for work elsewhere, and we encouraged her in that goal. I had hoped she would eventually join the company, but thought it would be wise for her to gain some helpful experience with another good company and then come to work with us later. When a suitable job did not materialize, however, I invited her to jump right in and work with us, hoping she would work her way through the ranks.

Nancy was not without experience: while still at UNC-W, she had started a clothing and accessories import business with another student. They traveled to Guatemala to source unique products for import to the U.S. She developed a marketing plan to sell the items to surf shops and boutiques on the southeastern coast. After graduating, she sold her part of the business to her partner.

Nancy began at Bob Barker Company with an entry-level sales position and was quite successful in growing her territory. Later, she became the training director, providing company-wide training designed to improve communications, problem solving, and quality control, as well as management training. Within two years, Nancy had become distribution manager, taking over responsibility for shipping, receiving, processing returns, managing inventory, and maintaining good relationships with our freight carriers.

Nancy briefly left the company to further her education and improve her skills by attending the Fuqua School of Business at Duke University. Pat also decided to study for an MBA at Duke, though she attended classes at night. The school was quite proud of having a mother and daughter in their program at the same time.

While Nancy was studying at Duke, she completed a summer internship at IBM's personal computer division in Research Triangle Park. That gave her some valuable experience with a major corporation.

After completing her degree, Nancy returned to Bob Barker Company, where she served as a project manager from 1997 to 1999. The biggest of those projects was leading the construction of our new 200,000 sq. ft. manufacturing and distribution facility in Fuquay-Varina, which was a major undertaking.

In conjunction with the new building, Nancy led a team to select and implement a more efficient warehouse management system, including some automation. When we ran into serious problems with a new software system designed for that purpose, Nancy stuck with it and led her team to work through the problems until we switched to a new system and got everything sorted out. Both the hardware and the facility have been key to our ability to turn orders around within 24 hours.

> Nancy Barker – *After we gave up on the JD Edwards software, we had to conduct a very short search for a replacement*

accounting package and warehouse management system. I helped select Exceed for warehouse management, which we used until 2012. That was quite an adventure: I was pregnant during that time and Rachel was born seven weeks early, so we had to transition the project leadership very suddenly.

From 1999 to 2001, Nancy served as an executive vice president for the company. My goal was for Nancy to eventually assume the role of president from me, so we had her work on a variety of projects in different areas of the business. During that time, she implemented a bottom-up budgeting process as well as call center metrics designed to improve our performance and efficiency, with notable results. A key to her successful development was the dedication of two of our top non-family executives: Nancy Mills and Ben Forbes mentored Nancy throughout her tenure as president.

I officially turned over the reins to Nancy on September 17, 2001. It was just a few days after the infamous terrorist attacks that destroyed the World Trade Center and the world was still vibrating with the repercussions of it. When we announced the transition on a preplanned date, I made a point of saying that we would not allow terrorists to disrupt our work, and that we would proceed with business as usual.

Nancy served as president until 2005, and performed admirably. During her tenure, she helped to transition the day-to-day operations of the business from me to others throughout the organization. She also recruited independent directors to the company's board, which was a major and important step for us. This smooth transition allowed the company to continue to grow and thrive as Pat and I have stepped out of the day-to-day running of the business.

> Nancy Barker – *When I had become president, I thought we needed to add independent directors to help with the transition. Mom and Dad were kind in their praise to me, but didn't give me much feedback for improvement. The independent directors were able to provide a more objective evaluation for performance as well as for determining appropriate salaries for our top-level employees.*

Before becoming president, Nancy had married Daniel C. Johns, and while she was running the company she was also giving birth to two daughters, Rachel and Adelle. Rachel was born just as Nancy was leading the implementation of our new Warehouse Management System. Adelle came along about three years later, after Nancy had become president. Ultimately, Nancy felt a need to devote more time to her family, so she left the role as president in 2005, turning it over to her brother Robert.

When Nancy's youngest daughter began kindergarten in 2008, she once again became hands-on in the business, returning as vice-president for marketing. In this role, she directed teams to explore several new market opportunities. As some of those grew into successful initiatives, Nancy began to focus her time on new opportunities and assumed the new role of Vice President for New Market Development. In this role, she led two teams to grow the business in electronic monitoring and officer supplies.

In January of 2012, Nancy led us in another direction, taking on a new position as Vice President for Corporate Social Responsibility. We have always tried to be good citizens who not only ran a profitable business but gave back to our employees, our community, and our world. Nancy is leading us to a new level in this area, developing a strategic plan for the company's impact on the environment, workplace, community and industry.

Robert

While Nancy jumped right in after college, our son Robert was more hesitant about joining the company. He wanted to try his hand in a venture of his own before throwing in his lot with the family business, and we fully supported him in that.

Robert was always a serious student who loved learning. He consistently took advanced classes in high school, and was actively involved in a variety of challenging extracurricular activities, including filmmaking.

Robert went on to the University of North Carolina, where he excelled in his freshman year, leading to an opportunity to study abroad at The London School of Economics. As a junior, he was accepted at the renowned Wharton School at the University of Pennsylvania, where he earned a Bachelor of Science in Economics with a dual concentration in Finance and Entrepreneurial Management in 1993, and was a *summa cum laude* graduate.

After college, Robert tried his hand in the restaurant business, developing a project he had begun in school.

He opened a casual restaurant featuring healthy food in Chapel Hill, calling it "The Healthy Bite." The demographics in Chapel Hill appeared to be ideal, and he put a lot of work into it. In time, however, Robert decided that the restaurant business was not something he wanted to do for the rest of his life, so he came back to work at the company in 1996.

> Robert Barker, Jr. – *When I started the Healthy Bite in Chapel Hill, it was based on a business plan from one of my entrepreneurial business classes. I wanted it to be a model business that offered healthy food at good value to customers while also treating our employees well. The restaurant business is a tough business, though: you couldn't really compete on a level playing field and still pay employees well. With a workforce consisting mainly of college students there was tremendous turnover, and finding employees who would dependably show up for work was difficult. I ran the restaurant for about two years, then sold the equipment and remaining lease to another restaurant.*

When Robert returned, we put him to work as Strategic Planning Director. Robert helped us develop the company's first three-year strategic plan, and we quickly saw the value of forward thinking.

From the end of 1996 to 2000, he put his computer skills to work by serving as the Information Technology (IT) manager, a tenure that became rocky when a promising ERP (Enterprise Resource Planning) software package turned out to be a disaster. Robert didn't make that decision alone, but he took a lot of heat for it.

About that time, Robert decided to leave the company for a while. He moved to San Francisco, hoping to learn more about Internet-based businesses, and perhaps to start one of his own. The timing was bad, however: the "dot.com" bubble burst just as he was trying to get started, and a career there did not materialize.

While in San Francisco, Robert helped us try to commercialize a biometric smart card fingerprint reader for use in detention centers – an added level of security that would enable only certain persons to open doors, for example. We invested in the company that was developing the smart card and worked on the project for about a year, but our partner company never produced a marketable product.

Robert moved back and rejoined the business in 2002. He served first as sales and marketing manager of our Barker Built division, which manufactured our metal detention equipment and furniture. Later, he became fully responsible for leading that division. Years later, however, as market conditions changed, he recognized that it would be more economical for us to subcontract all of our metal work. Choosing to shut down the manufacturing end of that division was a difficult but necessary business decision, and he had the unenviable responsibility for overseeing the transition and downsizing some fine employees.

Robert went on to serve as marketing director for a while, then became Vice President of Marketing. When Nancy decided to step down from the presidency, she talked privately with Robert about his interest in taking over the position. I think it came as a surprise to him, but he was both willing and capable, and when she left he became president of the company.

Robert has proven to be an outstanding executive. The company has advanced and grown under his leadership, and his tenure started with a real bang. One of our major competitors was a Utah-based company named Leslee Scott, and its president, Evan Trommer, approached Robert in 2005. Trommer was working with a private equity group to provide financing, and was interested in buying our business. Robert's response was that the Bob Barker Company was not for sale, and he soon turned the tables, negotiating to buy their business and expand our reach.

After six to nine months of negotiations, Robert led a merger and acquisition of Leslee Scott, and managed to do so while getting married to Jennifer Laws, in March 2006 – just one month before the acquisition was complete. He and Jennifer now have two sons, Robert J. Barker, III, and Raymond Barker.

Robert had his work cut out for him: merging the two operations and shifting our West Coast warehouse from California to Leslee Scott's Utah-based facility was a major undertaking. Integrating the computer systems in late 2006 was a real chore, and consolidating two product lines into one took longer that we thought. Our first sales catalog after the merger was planned for January of 2007, but it didn't go out until March.

Transitioning Leslee Scott employees into our company also took some extra effort. Some duplicate positions were eliminated, and downsizing employees is always painful. In the days when we were doing a lot of manufacturing, we had as many as 397 employees, but with less onsite manufacturing and greater automation, we currently have fewer than 200.

There was stress at the executive level, too. As part of the acquisition agreement, Evan Trommer received five percent of the company stock and came to work for us full time. Having previously been CEO of his company, however, he found it stressful to work as an employee. In 2007 he sold his stock and shifted to a part-time consultant role, which was a better fit for all concerned.

As he continues to lead the company, Robert is always learning and looking for ways to make the company even stronger, which bodes well for the future.

Passing the torch

When Pat and I incorporated the business in 1987, while Nancy and Robert were still in high school, we decided to make them partners in the company, with some ownership. We hoped, of course, that they would want to take over the business one day.

Leslee Scott's offer in 2005 was not the first time someone else had sought to buy the Bob Barker Company. In 2002, Pat and I were thinking about retiring, and wanting some financial security, we had seriously considered selling the company. There was significant interest from potential buyers, and Robert came back from San Francisco to participate in the discussion as we considered various aspects of these matters.

One night, after a group of investment bankers had left, we were sitting around the kitchen table when our CPA asked Robert and Nancy why they didn't consider buying the remainder of the business from us. They hadn't thought of that, but since they already owned more than half of the business together, the CPA explained that it would be possible for them to leverage enough money to purchase the remainder of the company from us.

The CPA warned us, however, that if we sold our shares in the business, we'd have to step back and let Robert and Nancy run it, because they would be the ones taking the financial risk. We had confidence in both Nancy and Robert, and in our ability to work together in an appropriate fashion, offering advice when asked but leaving major decisions to them.

We soon reached an agreement to sell. Nancy and Robert were able to borrow the funds needed, and in 2003 they purchased our part of the business except for two percent that Pat retained. Furthermore, they did so on the same terms the private equity firms had agreed to pay, so they felt good about paying us an appropriate amount. This provided the financial security that Pat and I needed for retirement, and the business successfully passed to the second generation.

Robert and Nancy have followed our pattern by passing on shares to their children, as well. Statistics suggest that not many family-owned businesses survive to a third generation of family leadership, but we are working and hoping that we can prove to be an exception to the rule.

> Robert Barker – *To buy the business, we had to borrow millions of dollars from Wachovia Bank, even though we already owned a meaningful part of the company from earlier grants Mom and Dad had made. Nancy and I have tried to do the same thing with our children, giving enough stock to the third genera-*

tion so they can one day buy us out and take it over if they want to. It's a given I think, that some children will be interested and others will not, so we're trying to set it up so they can buy shares from each other, and ultimately those involved with the business would have a greater say so than those who aren't.

CHAPTER **12**

Leaving a Legacy

I come to this chapter with a lot of nervousness. While quotes by employees that my co-author has scattered throughout the book are sometimes funny stories told at my expense – which I enjoy as much as anybody – many of those included here are so flattering that I fear coming across as vain or self-serving. I appreciate the kind words offered by these friends and have been persuaded to leave the quotes in, but I'd like readers to know it wasn't my idea.

I don't want to promote myself, but I do want my life to make a difference. Pat and I have always believed that we are part of a larger world, and we want our lives to count for something beyond personal enjoyment. We believe the same should be true about the Bob Barker Company, so we've tried to build a company that leaves a legacy not only for our family and our employees, but for the larger community.

Values

I have always believed in being an honest businessman who operates with integrity and concern for others, both customers and employees. I operated for years on a sense of knowing and doing what I felt was right, but as our company grew and we continued to add employees, I realized that we needed something more concrete. Pat and I read a lot of books and attended a number of business-related seminars in order to learn more about effective strategies for leading and maintaining a desired corporate culture.

Business gurus commonly emphasized the importance of having a company statement of vision, mission, and values. So, in the mid-1990s we did some brainstorming and came up with the following mission statement:

> *Our mission is to operate an ethical, innovative, and profitable business which meets the needs of our customers with maximum value products and superior services, while challenging employees with optimum opportunities for personal fulfillment, growth, advancement, and economic security.*

To that mission statement, we added a list of values that we dubbed the Bob Barker Company's "Ten Commandments," affirming our desire for every employee to follow these guidelines:

1. *Meet the needs of our customers first.*
2. *Strive for exceptional quality.*
3. *Work together as a team.*
4. *Work efficiently to cut costs.*

5. Think through every decision.
6. Communicate effectively within the company.
7. Address all problems immediately.
8. Act ethically and legally.
9. Set high goals.
10. Exercise autonomy with responsibility.

Our first mission statement and the "Ten Commandments" served us well for some time, but such documents should always be subject to revision as the years go by. Though we've never wavered from the basic principles and values with which we began, we expanded them somewhat in 2007, when we adopted a vision statement to go with a revamped version of our previous documents.

Our vision statement declared that

> *Bob Barker Company is the worldwide leader delivering innovative supplies and services to correctional and rehabilitation customers.*

That statement, brimming with confidence, did not express hope that we could become the leader, but affirmation that we were the leading company in the detention business, and we needed to live up to that position.

We also tweaked our mission statement to give it a more active stance:

> *At Bob Barker Company, we excel through world-class customer service, supply chain management, manufacturing and distribution. We are dedicat-*

ed to our employees and offer an ethical work environment with opportunities for intellectual growth, personal fulfillment, advancement and economic security. We view every experience as a possibility for growth, fostering an innovative and creative business environment.

Finally, the company's "Ten Commandments" were restated verbatim, but under the more coordinated heading "Value Statements" rather than "Ten Commandments."

The most recent revision of our guiding documents is shorter than previous versions, but more specific in stating that our desire goes beyond making a profit and operating a sustainable business: we want to serve God as well as our customers and employees. More than that, we want to do more than make a living from our business – we want our business to contribute to the living of those we serve.

Our vision, mission, and values statements are now briefly stated as follows:

Vision: Transforming criminal justice while honoring God in all we do.

Mission: By living our values and pursuing Bob's passion for customer service and innovation, we are creating profitable growth and positively impacting lives.

Values: Integrity, Service, Excellence, Innovation, Unity.

We have these statements, superimposed over a full-length photograph of me, framed and posted in various locations throughout our company offices, warehouse, and manufacturing areas. But we've added another document, too, a "Code of Conduct" for all of our employees. The code stresses the importance of doing our work with passion, confidence, teamwork, communication, and accountability to each other. We also have this Company Code of Conduct posted in our workspaces, promoting the following beliefs and behaviors:

Can do approach in overcoming roadblocks to achieve commitments. There is always a way.

Honor bound to work as a unified and effective team that promotes constructive team and individual behavior.

Promote the growth of every individual and success of the team.

Foster spirited, open, constructive, and respectful discussions aimed at finding the best solutions.

The threats to our livelihood are external – our ability to overcome them depends on being internally aligned, mentoring each other, and holding each other accountable.

Foster open – honest – two-way communications with all associates – taking personal responsibility for effectively promoting a consistent and accurate message delivered and heard.

These generic principles could work for a variety of businesses. In our company, they relate specifically to employees being not only committed to our values, but knowledgeable about our products and our process. Thus, we're constantly training employees, evaluating our procedures, and striving for improvement: the practical outworking of the general principles.

Working in this way, we have achieved a service level of 95 percent, meaning that 95 of every 100 product lines we carry is available to ship complete, and within 24 hours. Our intent is to be the gold standard of the corrections industry, by which all others are measured. We want our customers to know us as reliable, prompt, forthright, and properly informed regarding product availability and our ability to meet our customers' needs on time. We know that our customers have many other concerns: once they place an order with us, we don't want them to have to worry about it again.

Insights

As our company proved itself to be firmly grounded and successful for the long haul, I have been given many opportunities to speak to students and others who have an interest in business.

My first word of advice has to do with passion: you have to be excited and passionate about your work if you're going to truly enjoy it and succeed. I believe the two go together: I love going to work, and I'm sure that has contributed to my success. People who dislike what they're doing will not have the dedication, discipline, and perseverance needed to keep going through tough times and achieve their goals. I tell would-be entrepreneurs that if you can't find something that turns you on when planning your vocation, you'd better change it immediately, or you will not be successful. In more colloquial terms, "Find your passion early in your career, and stick to it like a hound dog on the scent of a deer."

Men and women who succeed in business have to be more than passionate, however: they also have to be innovative and creative, always looking for new products, new markets, or new opportunities. We've been successful in part because I've always sought to understand my customers' needs and then find or create the products that will make their jobs easier.

When I learned how hard it was to keep prisoners from turning everyday items into weapons, we developed short-handled or flexible toothbrushes that couldn't be turned into shivs, and designed razors that break apart so the handle can't be shaped into a shank. When I learned how many ways inmates have found to hide contraband, we developed shampoo and even toothpaste that is completely clear, and packaged in a clear bottle or tube.

Over the years we have registered many patents and developed hundreds of innovative products that have kept us in front of the field. I dare to say that Bob Barker Company changed the way business is transacted in the detention marketplace. Business people also have to be flexible. Economic factors change as interest rates go up or down, and as customers have more or less money to spend. Market conditions change, as manufacturing costs soar in one place while dropping in another. You can't be wedded to the notion of always doing things the same way. Computers were limited mainly to researchers and the military when I started the Bob Barker Company, but I can't imagine trying to operate without them today. The Internet was still science fiction back then, but today no national business can operate without an effective and interactive Website.

We cut our teeth on catalogs and still use them, but we knew that if our customers couldn't view and order their products online, we'd get left behind, so we invested in *bobbarker.com* as a first-rate and highly functional Web site. We've also wised up to the importance of social media: Bob Barker Company has a Facebook page, tweets new products or ideas on Twitter, and connects with business professionals on LinkedIn.

Sometimes, being flexible can call for hard decisions. In the course of building our business, for example, there was a time when we needed to develop a strong cut and sew manufacturing arm so we could ensure both quality and affordability, but over the years the global economic and trade landscape has changed. To remain competitive, we had to cut back on domestic production and find overseas sources for our products. Now our manufacturing is limited mainly to mattresses and vinyl products in which we have particular expertise or proprietary patents.

No matter how much external factors change, however, there are some basic principles that every successful businessperson needs to know and follow. Here are a baker's dozen of the ideas I've offered to young entrepreneurs who want to start a business:

1. *Evaluate your interests and talents* – realistically evaluate your abilities and your level of excitement about different options.
2. *Determine your niche* – the most successful businesses find an unmet need, and fill it better than anyone else. If your business or your products don't have a market, you won't be successful.
3. *Determine how you can make or provide your product to customers better than your competition* – if you're just one more business doing the same thing, you won't go far. What can you do that will set your company apart?
4. *Have a sound business plan* – how much will it cost to begin? How will you find the needed financing? How can you be assured of a return on your investment?
5. *Set goals* – businesses don't succeed by accident. They prosper when led by people who know where they want to go and set high but realistic goals as a target.
6. *Strive to attain those goals* – goals alone won't get you where you need to go: they have to be supported by sweat, determination, and a willingness to do what has to be done.
7. *Stay alert and knowledgeable of*

your business and the market – never assume that you have it all figured out: if you get caught napping or think you have "arrived," your competitors will leave you in the dust.

8. *Always remember your customers and their needs* – customers will do business with companies they trust to provide them the best combination of service and value. Where there are no customers, there is no business.
9. *Stay enthusiastic and passionate about your work* – if you lose your passion for the business, try your best to rejuvenate it. If you can't do that, sell the business or turn it over to other leaders, and find something else that makes your heart sing.
10. *Be creative, inventive, and innovative* – that requires a lot of effort, but it's the only way to stay out front.
11. *Motivate co-workers, employees, and associates* – very few businesses are one-man or one-woman operations. Effective leaders succeed because they are effective motivators. They know how to encourage, challenge, and reward others with whom they work.
12. *Don't be afraid of hard work or change* – the first is indispensable, the second is inevitable. Be prepared for both, and meet them head-on.

13. *Follow your dream* – you can make it become reality if you keep on keeping on. I am convinced that if you can dream it, if you can visualize it, you can do it.

Contributions

To the above list, I could have included another item: "give back." Life isn't just about us, or about how much money we can make. I believe that all businesses should strive to better the lives of their employees, contribute to their communities, and work for the greater good.

We want our employees to feel needed and valued, and we encourage them to excel in everything they do. We offer incentives for them to further their education, for example. Many of our employees who dropped out of school have now completed their GED through in-house tutoring programs, while others take educational coursework at surrounding schools and colleges to improve their skills. Bob Barker Company is a family-owned business, and we want everyone who works for us to feel like they are part of the family.

In addition to paying them a good wage, we show concern for employees' welfare by providing retirement benefits, health and life insurance, profit sharing, and vacation time. We show our appreciation through parties, luncheons, picnics, and company contests. We've contributed to our employees' well being by providing health fairs, smoking cessation programs, weight loss classes, and free or discount gym memberships. We've provided bonuses for workers who quit smoking or who achieve a healthy weight loss.

> Melba Richardson – *My sister works here – she's been here 15 years – my mom used to work here, my aunt worked here ... so it is a family-oriented company.*
>
> David McKinnon – *One of the main reasons the company has grown like it has, I believe, is the way you treat your people. I think that's the most important thing, the way you treat your people. That's one of the reasons I've been here so long, because they've always treated me good, every last one of them.*

All in all, we want Bob Barker Company to be a fun place to work, a place where employees feel valued and cared about. We want them to look forward to coming to work, knowing that they will find a strong support system and a joyful place to be.

We also encourage our employees to be involved in the local community by taking a leadership role in improving the quality of life for those around us. I've always supported the Chamber of Commerce, the Rotary Club, and other organizations, often serving as president or in other roles. I served as mayor of Apex from 1967-69 as a young man, and three decades later, after we had been in Fuquay-Varina for a while, I served that town as mayor from 1995-1999.

You could say that salesmanship is leadership, or that leadership is salesmanship: if you want to lead someone else to do something, you must first sell them on yourself by setting an example so they'll understand the importance of what you want them to do. Our company contributes regularly to local schools, civic events, and church activities, and we encourage our employees to do their part, too.

> William Stewart – *Even when you're outside the company, people see your shirt and your badges, and they say 'You work for the Bob Barker Company!' People know how much you do for the community ... Bob's name is really out there, and it's always positive. It makes you feel good to work for a company like this.*

> Pamala Williams – *I've learned a lot from Bob about always treating people with respect. He has never met a stranger. I've seen him give so much to help others, including me, or even people who stopped by the office and said they couldn't pay the light bill. I want people to know his heart. Bob has done so much for our community, from helping schools to businesses. Bob served two years as president of the Fuquay-Varina Chamber of Commerce and when it was about bankrupt, he took hold of that and got people in the community involved, and now it's thriving. He led the Varina Broad Street revitalization – there's just no end to what Bob has done for the community.*

A large part of my community involvement has been tied up with Campbell University, my alma mater. I've served on the Presidential Board of Advisors and the University Board of Trustees, including a stint as chair. One of my more exciting projects was acting as chair of the campaign cabinet charged with raising $30 million dollars for a badly needed convocation center and basketball arena. The experts thought it would take us five years to do it, but I believed we could do it in two years, and with a lot of work, we accomplished that goal. Today, the John W. Pope Jr. Convocation Center and the Gilbert Craig Gore arena are playing a vital role in helping Campbell University fulfill its mission of educating men and women in a Christian environment for service around the world.

On more than one occasion we have donated property or funds for special projects, because we believe in the school and its mission. If you visit Campbell University today, you'll see not only a fine dormitory named Bob Barker Hall, but a beautiful football facility named Barker-Lane stadium, a project to which my dentist friend and sometimes real-estate investment partner Don Lane also contributed.

But Campbell has been good to me, too. I considered it an honor to serve in those various ways, and was really flattered in May 2012 when the university recognized both Pat and me by conferring honorary Doctor of Humane Letters degrees on us.

My family has also been a strong supporter of the church. In 1985 we joined a handful of other volunteers as founding members of Woodhaven Baptist Church in Apex, where Pat and I remain active. We take a lot of joy in being part of a congregation that provides ministry opportunities both locally and abroad. We've enjoyed serving the church in a variety of roles, from working in the nursery to participating in mission trips, supporting fund-raising campaigns, and hosting church fellowships at our property on the Cape Fear River.

In recent years we have made a greater effort to give back through social responsibility and through improving the prison system. Our daughter Nancy now gives full time to that endeavor through her position as Vice President for Corporate Social Responsibility. Among other responsibilities, she oversees our charitable giving and seeks to ensure that our contributions go to agencies or groups that will use them responsibly in meeting important needs.

We've also become more focused on the people without whom we'd have no business: those who have been incarcerated for one reason or another, and need supplies. We believe our products help to make life better for inmates while they are in prison, but we also want to help improve their lives after they are released. For this reason we started the Bob Barker Company Foundation, with the vision of reducing recidivism by seeing lives of incarcerated individuals change forever through service to God, family, and community.

We believe these efforts are not only the right and responsible thing to do, but that they are making a difference. As the Bob Barker Company enters and passes beyond our 40th year, we intend to leave a legacy not only of success, but of service.